The Asian Jesus

The Asian Jesus

Michael Amaladoss, SJ

ORBIS BOOKS

Maryknoll, New York 10545

Founded in 1970, Orbis Books endeavors to publish works that enlighten the mind, nourish the spirit, and challenge the conscience. The publishing arm of the Maryknoll Fathers and Brothers, Orbis seeks to explore the global dimensions of the Christian faith and mission, to invite dialogue with diverse cultures and religious traditions, and to serve the cause of reconciliation and peace. The books published reflect the opinions of their authors and are not meant to represent the official position of the Maryknoll Society. To obtain more information about Maryknoll and Orbis Books, please visit our website at www.maryknoll.org.

Manufactured in the United States of America.
Manuscript editing and typesetting by Joan Marie Laflamme.

Permission to reprint the lyrics of "The Lord of the Dance" by Sydney Carter on pages 151-52, ©1963 Stainer & Bell, Ltd., Administered by Hope Publishing Co., Carol Stream, IL 60188, is gratefully acknowledged.

Cover art by the Sri Lankan artist Nalini Marcia Jayasuriya, *Christ* from *A Time for Singing: Witness of a Life*, page 56 © OMSC publications, New Haven, Connecticut, 2004. Reproduced with permission. "Rejoice with me, for I have found my sheep that was lost" (Luke 15:6).

Library of Congress Cataloging-in-Publication Data

Amaladoss, M. (Michael), 1936–
    The Asian Jesus / Michael Amaladoss.
        p. cm.
    Includes bibliographical references and indexes.
    ISBN-13: 978-1-57075-661-0 (pbk.)
    1. Typology (Theology) 2. Jesus Christ—Person and offices. 3. Asia—Religion.
I. Title.
    BT225.A53 2006
    232.095—dc22

                                                        2006012376

To

Jamels James

Contents

Acknowledgments

I wish to acknowledge the help that I have received from many people in developing this book over many decades. A complete list would be impossible. I can only refer to a few more significant, for me, persons. The pride of place would go to Fr. Ignatius Hirudayam, who triggered an interest in Indian culture—music, philosophy, and spirituality—when I was in the novitiate of the Society of Jesus (1954). This was nourished later by contacts with teachers like Fr. George Gispert-Sauch of Vidyajyoti, Delhi, and gurus like Swami Abhishiktananda. More recently I have been receiving encouragement from the team at Voies de l'Orient in Bruxelles, Belgium. Further, my work at the East Asian Pastoral Institute at Manila has widened my interest thanks to contact with people from all over Asia. The Institute of Dialogue with Cultures and Religions, Aikiya Alayam, Chennai, where I am now, has deepened the interest. The first version of this little book was read and commented on by Frs. Adolfo Nicolas (Japan-Manila), S. Arokiasamy (Delhi), P. R. John (Innsbruck), and Sr. Rekha Chennatu (Pune). I am grateful to all of them, especially to Fr. S. Arokiasamy, for their critical and encouraging observations. Many thanks to Fr. Francis Xavier, the provincial of Madurai Jesuit Province, for encouraging me to publish this book. I am grateful to Orbis Books and its editorial team for this edition of the book. It is now up to the readers to develop their own images of the Asian Jesus so that they can become more like him in their lives and relationships.

Introduction

Jesus was born, lived, preached, and died in Asia. Yet he is often seen as a Westerner. By historical circumstances Christianity spread more toward the West than the East.[1] That area coincided with the extent of the Roman Empire influenced by Greek culture and the Roman political and legal system. Some consider this providential. But this development cannot be used to impose Greco-Roman culture as normative for all Christians everywhere. The story of the apostle Thomas shows that some apostles may have ventured beyond the frontiers of the empire. Indians believe that Thomas came to India and was martyred in Chennai. The church of St. Thomas in India treasured its links with the church in Syria. Monuments witness to the fact that the Syrian Christians followed the trade routes and penetrated China in the eighth century of the Common Era. But the Syrian church was largely overrun by Islam. While it has continued a precarious existence, it has not developed very much. Its contact with India, for instance, has been infrequent. While the church in the Roman Empire had Western and Eastern wings, with their centers in Rome and Constantinople, respectively, Greek language and culture were their common medium.[2]

In modern times Jesus was brought to Asia by Western (Euro-American) missionaries and so has appeared Western. The missionaries came largely with the Portuguese colonizers in the sixteenth century. They imported an Euro-American church, unified and fortified in opposition to the Reformation, especially at the Council of Trent, with its liturgy, catechesis, theology, and ecclesiastical organization. The Asian reaction to this import, especially among the thinking and spiritual elite of Asia, especially in India, China, and Japan, was largely negative. In the nineteenth century the colonies became more stable political units, not exclusively trade-oriented outposts. An English-based educational system was fostered in India. This made interaction between Christianity and local cultures and religions possible. In non-colonized areas like China and Japan, Christianity did not make much headway. The Indians, though enslaved politically and economically, felt superior culturally and spiritually. At that time some Indian Hindus reacted to the Western Jesus by affirming that Jesus was really an "Oriental" and tried to reclaim his Oriental spiritual legacy. Many Indians even today would accept Jesus as their guru, though they would distance themselves from the church as an institu-

1

tion. Some Buddhist masters too have appreciated Jesus. The Dalai Lama and Thich Nhat Hanh of Vietnam have written books on Jesus. Bhikku Buddadasa of Thailand has introduced Jesus to the Thais in a series of lectures. But Jesus still remains largely Euro-American.

The Asian Bishops at the special Asian synod (1998) suggested images of Jesus that Asians today may find appealing: "the Teacher of Wisdom, the Healer, the Liberator, the Spiritual Guide, the Enlightened One, the Compassionate Friend of the Poor, the Good Samaritan, the Good Shepherd, the Obedient One."[3]

Some people may think that symbols and images are not adequate means of exploring the significance of the person and life of Jesus. They feel satisfied only with dogmatic formulas, even if they do not really understand them. The symbols and images do not aim at being condensed dogmatic statements. In order to avoid misunderstanding, I need to explain in the following pages my right to use the symbols and the way in which I am using them. It may sound like a defense. Yet I cannot avoid it under the present historical circumstances in the church. People who have no problem with images can move to the last paragraph of this introduction.

The Role of Images

What is the role of images in Christian faith and life? All images of Jesus arise in the context of the dialectic between his person and life and the life of the disciples. They answer the question: what does he mean to us today? They have double roots, one in his life as reported to us in the gospels and the other in the culture and history of the disciples, though one of these roots may be stronger in a particular image. For example, while the crucified Jesus is more rooted in his life, the Sacred Heart is more cultural.

Symbols and images are neither monopolistic nor exclusive. They are many. They point to different aspects or roles of the person. They are complementary. Every image may not speak to every person. People may prefer one or another image for historical, cultural, experiential, or personal reasons. An image may be limited. It may be inadequate to express the full reality of the person, taken by itself. An image is not a theological or a dogmatic affirmation, though it may be related both to theology and to dogma.

People who have an ontological frame of mind are often uncomfortable with images. They speak in absolutes and see images as relative. Let me take the image of prophet. If I say that Jesus is a prophet, I am pointing to the way he is challenging everyone to conversion in view of the reign of God, which he is proclaiming. But some people will not be happy unless I keep adding constantly that Jesus is the greatest prophet. He is more than other prophets. This is obviously a comparative affirmation. It is true, obviously, for a believer. But when I am exploring the prophetic dimension of the life, works, and teachings of Jesus, he will be similar to other prophets in some ways, different from them in others, and specific, even unique, in still others. I will have to bring this out too. But I need not be harping on such a comparison constantly. As a matter of fact, the uniqueness or specificity of Jesus may emerge precisely when many images of him are taken together. Muhammad is seen as a prophet by his followers. Others too may see him as having a prophetic charism that reformed the polytheistic and exploitative popular religions of Arabia of his time. The Muslims even look upon him as the final prophet, implying that he is the greatest. We Christians, of course, consider Jesus the ultimate prophet. But I can explore the role of Jesus as a prophet without comparing him constantly with other prophets. The specificity of Jesus as a prophet can be understood in its own terms without comparing him, much less opposing him, to other prophets. His specificity is who he is, not who he is not. The term *prophet* has a basic common meaning in itself. As such, it can be applied to different people in different situations, sacred and secular. It also acquires a specific meaning each time it is applied to a person. This specific meaning comes from the person to whom it is applied. These specific meanings can, of course, be compared. But they need not. In this book I am not engaged in comparative study. I just want to look at Jesus and understand his significance for Asia through symbols to which Asians are accustomed in their own cultural and religious traditions.

If I call Jesus a sage, I need not say that he is a sage like Confucius or that he is a better sage than Confucius. Sage is a symbol that is found in many cultures. It draws a certain common minimum content from these different cultures. I see Jesus in this context. But at the same time, exploring the life of Jesus, what he said and did, I can spell out what kind of sage Jesus was, what kind of special wisdom he communicates, and so forth. I can do this without a comparison between Jesus and Confucius or other sage figures of the Asian tradition like the Buddha or Tiruvalluvar. The image gives me only a framework, which is filled in by the identity of the person and work of Jesus. Depending upon my identity, if I am a Confucian, I may compare and contrast Jesus and Confucius as sages. If I am a Tamil, I may compare Jesus and Tiruvalluvar. But such comparisons are not necessary to understand Jesus as a sage, though they may throw more light on the specificity of Jesus. When two such sages encounter each other, what may be interesting is, not a comparison, but a dialogue. I do not, however, plan to engage in such a dialogue in this volume. Similarly, I can talk about Jesus as the way or *Tao*. My intention is not to determine, first of all, the exact meaning of *Tao* in the Chinese tradition and then apply it to Jesus and compare him as the way to *Tao*. Even a whole book will not be able to say the last word about the significance of *Tao* in the Chinese tradition and the different meanings given to that term in different branches of that tradition. When I call Jesus the way, rather, it is Jesus who gives a special meaning to the term *Tao*. At the same time, the term has the special resonance given to it by the Chinese tradition and it helps me to look at a particular dimension of the life and action of Jesus. I can do this without any comparison.

I can talk about Jesus as a guru. Everyone in India, perhaps even in the world, knows what a guru normally means. This image or symbol helps me to explore and understand some aspects of what Jesus is and does. The symbol guru has a particular significance in the Saiva Siddhanta tradition. I have no intention of exploring this and comparing it to Jesus as guru. One scholar, for instance, speaks of Jesus as the crucified guru.[4] The life and teaching of Jesus show me what kind of guru he is. This can be explored without any comparative study.

Images and Dogma

The language of symbols and images is not conceptual and logical. But it can be systematic. It gives rise to thought through interpretation, though we cannot lock it up in conceptual schemes. In a well-known phrase Paul Ricoeur said: "Symbols give rise to thought." Symbols are richer and more evocative than concepts. We Christians agree that Jesus is unique. But theologians still disagree about what this implies and involves in the way he functions in the history of salvation. What I am trying to say is that no one should find fault with symbolic language for not being conceptual or dogmatic. Loyalty to the faith of the church does not demand that we all repeat the same conceptual formulas. To privilege abstract, univocal concepts is to privilege the Greek cultural and philosophical tradition. I do not see why this should be. Neither concepts nor symbols are adequate to the mystery of the Divine. This is also true when we use them to speak about Jesus, who is divine and human. Before this mystery all that we can say is *neti, neti* (not this, not this). We see this process operative in the councils of the church. They are more busy denying heresies than in making positive affirmations. Let us not absolutize, then, any concepts or symbols. Only God is absolute. But we can talk about the Absolute only through our limited words, symbols, and concepts. We can set boundaries to our speech beyond which we cannot go, though we are very tentative about what we assert positively.

When we absolutize a symbol, it becomes an idol. A symbol is useful only insofar as it lead us to go deeper into the reality that it symbolizes. It has played its role well when it makes us aware that the reality transcends it in its individuality and depth. The symbol then becomes an icon that leads us to the contemplation of the mystery that it indicates.

Dogmatic affirmations are true. But they do not express the fullness of truth. Their expression can be limited by the situation in which they are made, the capacity and insight of the people making them, and the conceptual tools at their disposal. Exploring images, I am not developing a Christology in the traditional sense. No one image can pretend to present all aspects of the mystery of Jesus Christ. Image making is different from writing a treatise in systematic theology. Images, therefore, should not be judged in a theological framework. Images are rooted in the faith. They are pre-theological. They cannot be accused of not being theological. However, as symbols they can give rise to theological reflection. But the context of faith and life are always important. Symbols, taken singly or together, may not address all the concerns of a theological treatise. Symbols, therefore, should not be judged by comparing them to theological formulations. By perceiving Jesus as the way, the sage, or the guru, I cannot thrust into them the dogmatic formulas of Chalcedon or judge them in that context. This volume is not a theological treatise. It should be appreciated for what it says and should not be judged for what it does not say.

It is often said that one cannot speak of what Jesus is without saying what he does, that is, that he saves. The salvation that Jesus offers is such that it does not free us from the struggles and the efforts that we have to make in this life to live as saved humans. We are not spared the tensions and decisions. Salvation is not some mysterious, automatic, metaphysical activity. Jesus energizes and strengthens us to live as his disciples in this life. What it will be in the life after death we do not know except that we will be with him and with the Father and the Spirit, free of these struggles. Jesus as guru, for example, shows us the way to live as his disciples. Saying that he is divine or that he is savior may add depth but does not add anything to his role of being a guru in our lives. Rather, he saves me precisely by showing me the way to live as a person being saved and by enabling me to do so. He becomes a special kind of guru then. The process of salvation that theologians claim to explore is seen from a practical point of view in the images. Images are less concerned with metaphysics. They help us to live. I am taking for granted that he is divine, savior, and so on. I need not add all his attributes to every symbol that I explore. This does not mean that I deny them either. I am looking at Jesus as a guru without comparing him to other gurus. Even when the fathers tried to describe what Jesus was in the Council of Chalcedon, they made positive, not comparative, affirmations. They held the divine and human attributes of Jesus in tension without knowing how to integrate them.

Asian Images

In the following pages I would like to explore some Asian images of Jesus. I am not fool enough to think that I am the first Asian to do so. I am standing on the shoulders of many pioneers. I shall refer in a subsequent chapter to the images used by Asians of other religions, Hindus and Buddhists. Asian Christians also have used images. I only wish to make my own effort to look for images of Jesus in the context of Asia today. This context is one of cultural and religious pluralism. This will add to the pluralism of images.

I am exploring these images of Jesus as an Indian and as an Asian. I am an Indian. But at the same time I am also an Asian. I have some experience of the situations and cultures of Asia. I try to learn from them and enrich myself. I am aware, however, that if this effort were to be made by a Chinese or an Indonesian or a Japanese, it would be very different. The symbols can become objects for dialogue also within Asia. I am writing as a Christian. I am not engaging in an abstract comparative study. I do not pretend to stand outside the cultures and religions of Asia. But as an Indian and an Asian Christian I feel that Asian cultures and religions are not foreign to me. They are my heritage. They belong to my ancestors. I am in dialogue with them within myself. When an Indian image like guru is used, Hindus can claim it as their own, and Christians too may think of it as Hindu. While I do not deny its use in Hindu contexts, I think that it is more Indian than Hindu, being more cultural and linguistic than religious. As such, I feel that I have a right to use it in my own Indian Christian context. I do not have to apologize to anyone, nor do I need anyone's permission to do so. I can give it a Christian interpretation in my own religious context. It is true, however, that not all symbols used in a particular religious context are open to such reinterpretation. For example, if I speak of Krishna, Rama, or Siva, or symbols closely associated with them in Hindu myth and worship, I am obviously speaking in the context of Hinduism. It will not only be ambiguous but improper to use such names and symbols for Jesus. But a symbol like guru is not Hindu, but Indian, and common, though it is also used in Hindu religious contexts. Mateo Ricci and Roberto de Nobili in the seventeenth century pioneered such a distinction between religion and culture. So cultural symbols are available for use by people who belong to other religions. They may be adopted by people belonging to other cultures too. Similarly, avatar is a common symbol in a way that Krishna is not. I can call Jesus an avatar. I cannot call him Krishna. By calling Jesus avatar I am not comparing him to Krishna or to any other avatar. While avatar has a common significance, when I use the word for Jesus it acquires a specific meaning that is given to it by Jesus himself. The term or symbol acquires a new content. It is not really necessary to add further adjectives like *crucified*. Why not then the risen avatar, the saving avatar, the divine avatar, or all these adjectives in a string—the crucified, risen, saving, and divine avatar? Why not then attach this string of adjectives to every image and symbol? There is always a fear that some-one will say, "After all, Jesus is only a guru, like so many other gurus." Such a statement is made in a comparative context. There is also a prejudgment that the term *guru,* without further qualification, can only be used of a lim-ited human being. Every image used of Jesus need not evoke and express all that we can say about Jesus or all that he is. But it refers to a particular aspect of Jesus.

Some Indian Christians speak of Jesus as the *Adipurusha*—the primor-dial person. It is not a neutral symbol but carries with it the weight of the Vedic tradition, in which the *Adipurusha* has a special role in the process of creation. But as soon as I use an image like this to talk about Jesus, I am entering into a world of comparative philosophy/theology, which I am try-ing to avoid. I do not think that it is a suitable image for Jesus, not because it is Hindu, but because I do not want to be involved in the cosmology and anthropology that such an image evokes. People like Pandipeddi Chenchiah and Swami Abishiktananda use it in their exploration of the mystery of Jesus, but then it is set in the context of a particular theological anthropology, which needs to be explained and defended.

Talking in an intercultural, interreligious context, one cannot completely escape a certain comparative perspective. But I would like to keep this com-parison at the level of language and symbol and not get into the area of philosophical and theological reflection where it becomes comparative the-ology. I am not saying that comparative theology cannot or should not be done. I am only saying that I am not engaging in it here. I am exercising my right as an Indian and an Asian to speak of Jesus in my own language and culture and their symbols and images.

While I claim a right to use Asian images for Jesus and to dialogue with such images used in Asian cultures and religions, I shall refrain from such dialogue in this volume. As an Indian/Asian Christian I can carry on this dialogue within myself. But if I wish to give it expression, it may be good to do it in an interreligious and intercultural dialogical context where there are other interlocutors present. That is to say, I would prefer a Hindu to speak about the Hindu understanding of guru and a Confucian to explain the Chi-nese understanding of sage. Here I am just saying how, as an Asian Chris-tian, I am perceiving Jesus as a guru and a sage.

The emergence of images of Jesus in the New Testament and in the his-tory of the church justifies my effort. I am not engaged in any attempt to redefine the dogmas of the church. I certainly do not deny them. But I think that they do not say all that Christians could say about Jesus to make him meaningful to themselves and to others in different cultural and religious contexts. Images do not deny dogma but complement it at another level. They bring a new perspective that makes Jesus relevant to us today. Dogmas tend to limit themselves to the exploration of what Jesus is in his "ontological and personal" constitution in the context of heresies in the early centuries of Christianity. They may also represent a Greek cultural concern. Symbols focus rather on what Jesus does. Of course, what he does is not without an impact on what he is, though it brings out different aspects of his personality.

Who is my audience in this book? My audience is the ordinary believing Asian Christian. I assume a certain familiarity with the story of Jesus as it is narrated to us in the four gospels. The gospels use their own images. But beyond those images, which are already interpretative, there is a simple story of Jesus, his actions and teaching. I take for granted that this is known in a general way, so that my language is allusive at times. I do not feel the need to recount the story of Jesus. This means that this book is not primarily for members of other religions who do not know anything about Jesus. But a member of another religion who has some familiarity with the person of Jesus and his life and has a desire to understand more deeply his significance may find this book interesting. The second chapter gives some idea of how Hindus and Buddhists look at Jesus from their own religious context.

Talking of symbols and images we are working at a second level, one step removed from the simple act of narrating a story. Symbols give rise to interpretative reflection. Such reflection would be at yet another level.

Before I present my choice of Asian images of Jesus, I would like, first of all, to present rapidly the images of Jesus that have emerged in the Christian tradition. Then I shall evoke the images that Hindus and Buddhists in Asia have found for Jesus.

1

Images of Jesus in Christian History

How is it that an Asian Jesus becomes Western? Jesus was born a Jew in Palestine. He was baptized by John the Baptist. He proclaimed the coming of God's rule and called people to accept it. He explained its nature by many parables and spelled out its demands in many discourses. He illustrated and made real God's reign by his many miracles of healing. He announced God's forgiving and self-giving love and demonstrated it by his fellowship with the poor and the outcasts of his day. He was seen as a threat by Jewish authorities, who put him to death with the help of the Roman power. His disciples affirmed that he came to life again, and they went about the then-known world preaching Jesus and the reign of God that he inaugurated, calling people to become his disciples.

Jesus was no ordinary man. People who met him, saw his actions, and heard his preaching were forced to ask: "Who is this man?" Their answer to this question depended on two factors. One was their experience of him: what they saw and heard of what he did and said. The other was the context and culture from which they assessed his significance: "What does he mean to us?" Every one witnessed his miracles and listened to his discourses calling for a change of heart toward God and others. Some saw him as a rabbi who taught with authority principles and perspectives that looked revolutionary. Others saw him as a prophet who announced and realized the coming reign of God. A few even thought that he was the Messiah, whom they were expecting to come and reestablish Israel's kingdom. People like Herod saw him only as a miracle worker, though, for a moment, he was afraid that he might be another John the Baptist who would also condemn Herod's misdeeds. The Jewish leaders saw him as a pretender with a certain influence among the people, threatening and challenging their own power. His disrespect for the sabbath and his cleansing of the Temple upset them. Pilate mocked him as the "king of the Jews," whom he could crucify. Here we have different images of Jesus. Their sources are in the historico-cultural tradition of the Jews. The choice of a particular image depends on how a person or group relates to Jesus, their attitudes and perspectives.

The disciples, who followed and lived with Jesus, heard his teachings, and saw his miracles of healing and exorcism, thought that he was the Messiah whom they were expecting. The question that John the Baptist put to him through his disciples may be seen as paradigmatic:

> When John heard in prison what the Messiah was doing, he sent word by his disciples and said to him, "Are you the one who is to come, or are we to wait for another?" Jesus answered them, "Go and tell John what you hear and see: the blind receive their sight, the lame walk, the lepers are cleansed, the deaf hear, the dead are raised, and the poor have good news brought to them." (Matt 11:2–5)

With a reference to the prophet Isaiah, the answer of Jesus seems positive. He goes to the same text when he proclaims his identity in the synagogue at Nazareth. He reads:

> "The Spirit of the Lord is upon me,
>> because he has anointed me to bring the good news to
>>> the poor.
> He has sent me to proclaim release to the captives
>> and recovery of sight to the blind,
>> to let the oppressed go free,
> to proclaim the year of the Lord's favor." (Lk 4:18–19)

Then he announces: "Today this scripture has been fulfilled in your hearing" (Lk 4:21). We hear the same expectation from the disciples who were proceeding to Emmaus after the death of Jesus. They told Jesus himself, who was walking with them, unrecognized by them:

> "The things about Jesus of Nazareth, who was a prophet mighty in deed and word before God and all the people, and how our chief priests and leaders handed him over to be condemned to death and crucified him. But we had hoped that he was the one to redeem Israel. Yes, and besides all this, it is now the third day since these things took place. Moreover, some women of our group astounded us. They were at the tomb early this morning, and when they did not find his body there, they came back and told us that they had indeed seen a vision of angels who said that he was alive. Some of those who were with us went to the tomb and found it just as the women had said; but they did not see him." Then he said to them, "Oh, how foolish you are, and how slow of heart to believe all that the prophets have declared! Was it not necessary that the Messiah should suffer these things and then

enter into his glory?" Then beginning with Moses and all the prophets, he interpreted to them the things about himself in all the scriptures. (Lk 24:19–27)

Finally, when Jesus was with all the disciples together,

> they asked him, "Lord, is this the time when you will restore the kingdom to Israel?" He replied, "It is not for you to know the times or periods that the Father has set by his own authority. But you will receive power when the Holy Spirit has come upon you; and you will be my witnesses in Jerusalem, in all Judea and Samaria, and to the ends of the earth." When he had said this, as they were watching, he was lifted up, and a cloud took him out of their sight. While he was going and they were gazing up toward heaven, suddenly two men in white robes stood by them. They said, "Men of Galilee, why do you stand looking up toward heaven? This Jesus, who has been taken up from you into heaven, will come in the same way as you saw him go into heaven." (Acts 1:6–11)

Jesus Descending and Ascending

These texts provide us a background to understand how the early Christians arrive at their image of Jesus as Lord. The disciples had seen him as a prophet and the Messiah. He announced the reign of God and inaugurated it by his miracles of forgiveness and healing. They saw him arrested by the Jewish leaders and delivered into the hands of the Romans to be killed as a false messiah. But God justified him by raising him up to life again. The reign of God that Jesus proclaimed, however, had not fully come before Jesus was taken up to heaven. But what they had experienced assured them that Jesus was now with the Father and would come again to achieve God's reign on earth. Stephen declares before the Jewish leaders: "I see the heavens opened and the Son of Man standing at the right hand of God!" (Acts 7:56).

We need not speculate here on the process through which their experience of the life, death, and resurrection of Jesus coalesces into a composite image. But we see it in an early Christian hymn that Paul quotes in his letter to the Philippians:

> Let the same mind be in you that was in Christ Jesus,
> who, though he was in the form of God
>> did not regard equality with God as something to be
>>> exploited,
> but emptied himself, taking the form of a slave,

being born in human likeness.
And being found in human form,
he humbled himself
and became obedient to the point of death—
even death on a cross.

Therefore God also highly exalted him
and gave him the name that is above every name,
so that at the name of Jesus
every knee should bend,
in heaven and on earth and under the earth,
and every tongue should confess
that Jesus Christ is Lord,
to the glory of God the Father. (Phil 2:5–11)

This hymn has many parallels. The image it conveys is that of a divine being who descends to the earth, becomes human, suffers, dies, but is raised
up again and becomes Lord. Jesus is Lord. He becomes incarnate and suffers and dies through obedience to the Father's will. He is reestablished as
Lord through his resurrection. There is a process of descent and ascent that
is part of the history of the human world. It has therefore a double aspect:
what happens to him and what happens to the world. As far as the world
is concerned, this process is not complete. The reign of God has not been
fully established. So the Lord will come again to achieve it. As Paul says: "I
am confident of this, that the one who began a good work among you will
bring it to completion by the day of Jesus Christ" (Phil 2:16). This day of
Jesus Christ is obviously in the future. That is why the people continue to
pray: "Come, Lord Jesus!" (Rv 22:20). The image is not that of a human
being who is made divine by God. Rather, Jesus is a divine being who takes
on humanity and demonstrates his identity by his perfect obedience.

Jesus Is Lord

The early Christians experience and confess Jesus Christ as divine-human
Lord. Jesus is Lord! They worship him. They pray to him. The gospels evoke
the life and work of Jesus precisely to justify this faith vision. As John says
toward the end of his gospel: "These are written so that you may come to
believe that Jesus is the Messiah, the Son of God, and that through believing you may have life in his name" (Jn 20:31).

"Jesus is Lord!" This is the dominant image of the early church. But in
trying to justify it the gospels evoke other images. These are specified by the
historical, cultural, and theological contexts from which they were written.

Jesus in the Gospels

Mark starts with the affirmation that Jesus Christ is the "Son of God" (Mk 1:1). A heavenly voice confirms this when Jesus receives baptism at the hand of John the Baptist: "You are my son, the Beloved; with you I am well pleased" (Mk 1:11). But Mark seems to build his narrative around the idea of the messianic secret. Though Jesus expels evil spirits and heals people, he warns the beneficiaries not to speak about it. Though his life and actions, proclaiming the reign of God and calling for conversion, do raise questions about him, people in general do not recognize his messianic identity. Jesus reveals it only before the high priest (Mk 14:61–62) and is killed. His claim is justified by his resurrection.

For Matthew, Jesus is indeed the Messiah, who brings the new law fulfilling the old (Mt 5:17). He is a rabbi who teaches with authority. "You have heard that it was said . . . But I say to you" (Mt 5:21–22). He uses parables and discourses to convey his teaching. He preaches the new law of love from the heart—loving others, even our enemies (Mt 5:38–48), seeing himself in them, especially in the poor (Mt 25:31–46). He makes disciples and sends them everywhere to make other disciples (Mt 28:18–20). Matthew's audience seems to be primarily Jewish communities. He is trying to make them understand that Jesus is not the kind of messiah whom they were expecting. He is a messiah who is destined to suffer and to be killed.

Luke seems to be writing primarily to non-Jewish communities. He presents Jesus as the great reconciler and healer. He witnesses to the forgiving and reconciling love of God. His mission is set in the context of the jubilee, when all debts should be forgiven and all property restored to their original owners, so that the community starts anew (cf. Lv 25 and Dt 15). He brings good news to the poor, sight to the blind, and freedom to the captives (Lk 4:18–19). He also proclaims forgiveness to sinners. He speaks of the prodigal father who receives back his wayward son with unconditional love and of the good shepherd who goes after the lost sheep (Lk 15). Luke narrates the story of Zacchaeus, a tax collector who is converted (Lk 19:1–10).

John sees Jesus as the Word of God become flesh (Jn 1:1–14). The biblical "Word" indicates not merely revelation but also action. John's image of the Word may also depend on the biblical image of Wisdom, which is closely related to God and yet personified as a divine being in the Old Testament.

> The LORD created me at the beginning of his work,
>   the first of his acts of long ago.
> Ages ago I was set up,
>   at the first, before the beginning of the earth.

When there were no depths I was brought forth,
　　when there were no springs abounding with water.
Before the mountains had been shaped,
　　before the hills, I was brought forth—
when he had not yet made earth and fields,
　　or the world's first bits of soil.
When he established the heavens, I was there,
　　when he drew a circle on the face of the deep,
when he made firm the skies above,
　　when he established the fountains of the deep,
when he assigned to the sea its limit,
　　so that the waters might not transgress his command,
when he marked out the foundations of the earth,
　　then I was beside him, like a master worker;
and I was daily his delight,
　　rejoicing before him always,
rejoicing in his inhabited world
　　and delighting in the human race. (Prv 8:22–31)

This makes it easy for John to personify the Word as God's self-manifestation. God's self-manifestation in Jesus encounters the refusal of the Jews. John lays much stress on this confrontation. At the same time, the divinity of the Word is highlighted by the "I am" sayings: "I am the bread of life" (Jn 6:35); "I am the light of the world" (Jn 8:12); "Before Abraham was, I am" (Jn 8:58); "I am the good shepherd" (Jn 10:11); "I am the resurrection and the life" (Jn 11:25); and "I am the way, and the truth, and the life" (Jn 14:6). The Word, however, becomes flesh and therefore really human. This makes it possible for Jesus to raise humanity to divine status. Here we see the descending and ascending paradigm. Participation in divine life leads to communion with God and with others, shown in love and self-giving service (Jn 17). The vine and the branches become the symbol of this communion (Jn 15:1–13). The Spirit is given to sustain and strengthen this communion (Jn 14:15–17). Forgiveness is a dimension of this communion. After his resurrection Jesus appeared to his apostles and he "breathed on them and said to them, 'Receive the Holy Spirit. If you forgive the sins of any, they are forgiven them'" (Jn 20:22–23).

All the gospels give great importance to the suffering and death of Jesus. They refer back to the image of the Suffering Servant of Yahweh in Isaiah (Is 52:13—53:12). Jesus suffers for us,. The exact nature of the "for us," however, is not specified. It could be exemplary, inspirational, covenantal, and manifest solidarity and self-gift—everything except expiation and substitution. Total self-gift and surrender seem to be conditions for total acceptance and communion. There is no Jesus without the cross. This is the reason that Paul finds glory in the crucified Jesus (Gal 6:14).

Jesus as the High Priest

But the image of lord pushes all other images to the background. Even the passion is seen as a necessary passage to the Lord's glorification. During the persecutions this necessity is experienced also at a personal level as a participation in the Lord's sufferings. What dominates, however, is the lordship of Christ. The letter to the Hebrews is representative of this image:

> Long ago God spoke to our ancestors in many and various ways by the prophets, but in these last days he has spoken to us by a Son, whom he appointed heir of all things, through whom he also created the worlds. He is the reflection of God's glory and the exact imprint of God's very being, and he sustains all things by his powerful word. When he had made purification for sins, he sat down at the right hand of the Majesty on high, having become as much superior to angels as the name he has inherited is more excellent than theirs. (Heb 1:1–4)

This image of glory is complemented by the image of his humanity:

> Since, then, we have a great high priest who has passed through the heavens, Jesus, the Son of God, let us hold fast to our confession. For we do not have a high priest who is unable to sympathize with our weaknesses, but we have one who in every respect has been tested as we are, yet without sin. Let us therefore approach the throne of grace with boldness, so that we may receive mercy and find grace to help in time of need. (Heb 4:14–16)

This image of the glorious Christ will be perpetuated, not only in popular devotion, but also in the image of Christ, the Lord of all—*Pantocrator*—that can be seen above the main entrance to many early cathedrals. The liturgy of the Eastern church is also centered on the mystery of Christ the high priest interceding for us in heaven. It is this mystery that we celebrate and in which we participate.

The Jesus of Theological Reflection

The first councils of the church affirm that their belief in Jesus Christ as divine Lord is not against the biblical affirmation: "I am the LORD your God

. . . You shall have no other gods before me" (Dt 5:6). The Council of Nicea (325) affirms belief

> in one Lord Jesus Christ, the Son of God, the only-begotten generated from the Father, that is, from the being *(ousia)* of the Father, God from God, Light from Light, true God from true God, begotten, not made, one in being *(homoousios)* with the Father, through whom all things were made, those in heaven and those on earth. For us human beings and for our salvation he came down, and became flesh, was made man, suffered and rose again on the third day. He ascended to the heavens and shall come again to judge the living and the dead.

The Council of Chalcedon (451), on the other hand, confesses

> one and the same Son, our Lord Jesus Christ, the same perfect in divinity and perfect in humanity, the same truly God and truly man composed of rational soul and body, the same one in being *(homoousios)* with the Father as to the divinity and one in being with us as to the humanity, like unto us in all things but sin (cf. Heb 4:15) . . . in two natures, without confusion or change, without division or separation.

The councils affirm that Jesus Christ is both divine and human. They use some technical terminology. They do not explain the mystery. They lay down the boundaries of the language that speaks about it. They oppose both affirmations that emphasize one-sidedly the divinity or humanity of Jesus and statements that seek to subordinate Jesus to the Father. But these statements are very different from inspiring symbols and images.

Jesus, the King of Kings

In the Western church the image of Christ the Lord takes the form of the King of kings. After the conversion of Emperor Constantine, the whole empire becomes Christian—at least sociologically—and Christ is enthroned as the King of kings. This image continues to hold sway to this day. In the beginning the emperor is seen as his delegate on earth, ruling by his authority. He is seen not only as the head of the political kingdom but also of the church. The emperors called and presided over some of the early ecumenical councils. When the empire collapses, the pope succeeds to this role, enjoying sacred and secular authority, specified as the two swords of power. The pope consecrates and deposes kings. At the time of colonial expansion he can even divide the New World between Spanish and Portuguese spheres of influence. The liberation of science, philosophy, and political power from papal authority in Europe is the result of a long struggle—one of the reasons for the anti-clericalism and secularization in Europe. The colonial masters claimed the power to impose Christianity on people of other religions, even with military might when and where necessary. Scriptural justification for this practice was found in the phrase "Compel people to come in" (Lk 14:23), which Jesus puts in the mouth of the host in his parable of the Great Dinner (cf. Luke 14:12–24). The pope will continue to claim a certain universal authority in the spiritual realm as the vicar of Christ. Even today it is affirmed that everyone who is saved is related in some mysterious way to the church, whose visible head is the pope. The church still celebrates the feast of Christ the King. Images of Jesus with a golden crown are common. In popular religiosity even the child Jesus is seen with a crown.

Jesus on the Cross

In the early church, both in the East and in the West, people did not concentrate much on the passion of Jesus, though it is the centerpiece in all the gospels. Jesus instructs his disciples both before and after his death-resurrection that his way to glory passes through suffering. We have seen the path of descent and ascent in the hymns of the early church. Paul told the Corinthians: "When I came to you, brothers and sisters, I did not come proclaiming the mystery of God to you in lofty words of wisdom. For I decided to know nothing among you except Jesus Christ, and him crucified" (1 Cor 2:1–2). The Eastern church thought of salvation as participation in the divine life that Jesus, who comes down from heaven, shares with us. That was also the reason why it defended the divinity and humanity of Christ in the early councils. Because Jesus is really human, he can be one of us. But because he is also really divine, he can make us all divine, sharers of the divine life. The Western church, however, thought of salvation in more juridical terms. Whatever its theological explanation, the focus was on the fact that Jesus has saved us by suffering and dying for us. The sufferings of Jesus then become the manifestation of God's love for us. As Paul had said: "God proves his love for us in that while we still were sinners Christ died for us" (Rom 5:8). Images of the suffering Christ on the cross therefore became common in Europe. Devotions like the Way of the Cross became popular. To the images of the suffering Jesus were later added the image of the Sacred Heart. There is still a reference to suffering here, since the heart of Jesus is pierced. But the main image of the heart symbolizes love. The juridical attitude to the sufferings of Jesus is kept alive by the insistence on reparation. The image of the Sacred Heart of Jesus as an object of devotion is so common in places like India that when members of other religions seek to represent Jesus they seem to choose it spontaneously. The eucharistic body of Christ also becomes a common means of encountering Christ. The focus is on the presence of Jesus with us, though it also relates to his sacrificial self-offering. A common element underlying all these symbols seems to be a vertical relationship to Jesus, who is the king, who died for us, who loves and suffers for us, who is present to us in the form of bread. The attitude is one of adoration.

This attitude, however, changes in contemporary liberation movements. Jesus opts for the poor and struggles with them for their liberation. He is prophetically critical of the religious and political leaders of the time. They choose to do away with him. Jesus takes on the sufferings imposed on him in solidarity with the poor. Both the fact that, in Jesus, God suffers in solidarity with the suffering poor and the fact that, in the resurrection of Jesus, the good finally wins over the evil, are sources of strength and hope for the suffering poor. They assure us that God is with us, even if total liberation may be eschatological.

Jesus as the Word

The attention of the Reformers in the sixteenth century is on Jesus the Word. Jesus is the revealer. His revelation demands on our part the response of faith. This faith is justifying or salvific. Jesus as the Word of God challenges and judges us. He also saves us. But I have the impression that the focus of the reformed Christians moves slowly from Jesus the Word of God to the Bible as the written word of God. Reading the word and listening to it become important. Attempts are made to spread the word through the media. A certain automatic efficacy is even attributed to it. The life of Jesus or the New Testament slowly yields its place to the whole Bible. God and God's word overshadow Jesus. In the more recent Pentecostal groups the Spirit of God seems to replace Jesus as the center of attention, though sometimes we may not see a clear distinction between the Lord Jesus and the Spirit.

Jesus, the Liberator

In the latter part of the twentieth century Jesus was seen as the liberator, especially by the poor and oppressed Christians of Latin America, Africa, and Asia. When Jesus is seen as Lord, the focus is on the risen and glorified Jesus. Less attention is paid to the life, passion, and death of Jesus. The image of Jesus as liberator seeks to restore the balance. The poor look more closely at the life of Jesus and see that he actually preached good news to the poor. In a society that was divided between the rich and powerful elite and the poor and oppressed people, Jesus is critical of the self-sufficient rich and speaks and acts in solidarity with the poor. While he does not promote

a revolutionary movement, he does not shy away from the political sp....
in his opposition to the oppressors. He practices table fellowship with the
poor and the oppressed. His miracles address their needs, at least symbolically. He does not hesitate to suffer and die when the powerful leaders decide to remove him from the scene. His suffering and death can be seen as
gestures of protest on behalf of the poor. The reign of God that he proclaims
and delineates in his teaching provides the framework for a new society of
freedom, fellowship, and justice. In Jesus, therefore, the poor see God with
them, struggling with them and dying with them. The resurrection of Jesus
then becomes an assurance of liberation, even if this liberation remains an
object of eschatological hope. But the transformation that Jesus seeks to
bring is not merely for the next world. It becomes actively present already
in history wherever people love one another, share their goods, and serve
others even unto death. Through his disciples Jesus launches a social movement of liberation in history. They keep struggling for this liberation in collaboration with all people of good will.

A Hindu-Christian Jesus

Brahmabandhab Upadyaya (1861–1907) called himself a Hindu-Christian:
Hindu with regard to culture and Christian with regard to religion. He used
the term *Saccidananda* (*Sat* [truth] + *Cit* [consciousness] + *Ananda* [bliss])
to refer to the Trinity. He strongly affirmed the divinity of Jesus by identify-
ing him with *Cit*. He expressed his faith in Jesus in a hymn.

The transcendent Image of Brahman,
Blossomed and mirrored in the full-to-overflowing
Eternal Intelligence—
Victory to God, the God-Man.

Child of the pure Virgin,
Guide of the Universe, infinite in being
Yet beauteous with relations,
Victory to God, the God-Man.

Ornament of the Assembly
Of saints and sages, Destroyer of fear,
Chastiser of the Spirit of Evil—
Victory to God, the God-Man.

Dispeller of weakness
Of soul and body, pouring out life for others,

>Whose deeds are holy,
>Victory to God, the God-Man.
>
>Priest and Offerer of his own soul in agony,
>Whose life is Sacrifice,
>Destroyer of sin's poison,—
>Victory to God, the God-Man.
>
>Tender, beloved, soother of the human heart,
>Ointment of the eyes,
>Vanquisher of fierce death,—
>Victory to God, the God-Man.[1]

The hymn has to be heard in the original Sanskrit to catch all the allusions to Indian religious tradition and the resonance of Indian terminology like *Cit, Hari, Brahman, Saguna, Nirguna, Nara-Hari,* and so on. It is a litany of evocative symbols and attributes that at the same time make a theological point. It is the fruit of dialogue between two philosophical traditions but in deep and conscious fidelity to a single tradition of faith.

I have given a very rapid survey of some of the different images or names that Jesus has had through Christian history. This shows that the believers were not satisfied with a repetition of the dogmas of Nicea and Chalcedon to understand and live the significance of Christ in their lives.

2

Images of Jesus
among Other Asian Believers

Before I evoke some Asian Christian images of Jesus it will be helpful to see, very briefly, how other Asians have imaged Jesus. Even today, many Hindus who are critical of or even opposed to Christianity as a religion will have a soft corner for Jesus as a teacher, a guru, or an avatar, not only for Christians, but also for themselves. They would not accept the claims to uniqueness and superiority that Christians make about Jesus, considering him as God. But they have no problem in accepting Jesus as a "divine" figure. This is true of ordinary people as well as the educated elite and can be illustrated as a constant practice in India for over two hundred years. Some, like Gandhi, would claim to be his disciples. In the following pages I shall focus on a few people who have been articulate in their views about Jesus.

Jesus as a Moral Teacher

Raja Ram Mohan Roy (1774–1833) was a socioreligious reformer. He wanted to rid Hinduism of its superstitions like polytheism and "idol" worship. He also campaigned against social practices like the burning of the widows with their dead husbands. His zeal for religious reform also led him to criticize Christians who worshiped the Trinity instead of being strict monotheists or Unitarians. He must have been influenced by the Deist tradition in England. He tended to demythologize the gospel stories about Jesus, drawing from them only his precepts. He wrote to a friend in 1815:

The consequence of my long and uninterrupted researches into religious truth has been that I have found the doctrine of Christ more conducive to moral principles and better adapted for the use of rational beings than any others which have come to my knowledge.[1]

He compiled a volume, *The Precepts of Jesus,* in which he collected passages from the parables and sermons in the gospels. He wrote to another
friend:

> I regret only that the followers of Jesus, in general, should have paid
> much greater attention to enquiries after his nature than to the obser-
> vance of his commandments.[2]

He had, however, very definite views about the nature of Jesus. Because of
his strong monotheism, probably linked also to Indian non-duality *(advaita),*
he refused to accept Jesus as God. He spoke of the unity of will between
Jesus and God rather than of identity of being. People are saved not by the
death of Jesus but by being obedient to God by the faithful following of the
precepts of Jesus. In short, for Ram Mohan Roy, Jesus was an exemplary
human being who taught us how to live by word and example. He shows us
the way to self-discovery and moral behavior.

Jesus as Avatar

Ramakrishna Paramahamsa (1836–86) was a saintly figure in Bengal who
had a group of disciples. He was open to other religions, comparing them
to the different words used in different languages to indicate the same reality. He showed this openness in using resources from different religions for
his *sadhana* (spiritual effort). He was attracted to a picture of Mary with the
child Jesus that he saw in the house of one of his devotees. Shortly after this,
as he was walking in his garden,

> he saw an extra-ordinary looking person of serene aspect and foreign
> extraction approach gazing at him. Sri Ramakrishna's heart sponta-
> neously assured him that it was none other than Christ. The Son of
> Man then embraced him and merged in him, sending him to deep ec-
> stasy.[3]

What is significant here is the claim to experience Christ personally outside
the official mediations of the church. Ramakrishna considered Jesus as one
of the avatars. He seemed to have considered himself an avatar, and certainly
his disciples thought so.[4]

Swami Vivekananda (1863–1902) was Ramakrishna's favorite disciple and
founder of the Ramakrishna order of monks. The order was founded on
Christmas Eve, and Vivekananda spoke about Jesus and his life to the monks,
holding him up as an example to follow. The feast of Christmas is still celebrated every year in the houses of the order. Vivekananda considered Jesus

as an avatar or incarnation of God, but certainly not as the only one. He did not worry much about the historicity of Jesus. He thought that as an avatar, Jesus could not really suffer. So he did not take seriously the death and resurrection of Jesus and the aspect of redemption. As a matter of fact, he accepts ignorance (avidya) as an obstacle to self-realization, but not sin. What we call sin may indicate imperfection, but by encouraging guilt we only make the chains of ignorance stronger.

Jesus as an avatar experiences his one-ness or non-duality with the divine and is therefore a model for all of us to follow.

> Jesus had our nature; he became the Christ; so can we and so *must* we. Christ and Buddha were the names of a state to be attained. Jesus and Gautama were the persons to manifest it.[5]

One need not become a Christian to be a follower of Jesus.

> The Christian is not to become a Hindu or Buddhist, nor a Hindu or a Buddhist to become a Christian. But each must assimilate the spirit of the others and yet perceive his individuality and grow according to his own law of growth.[6]

The following passage gives an idea of how Vivekananda saw Jesus Christ:

> The Word has two manifestations, the general one of Nature, and the special one of the great Incarnations of God—Krishna, Buddha, Jesus and Ramakrishna. Christ the special manifestation of the Absolute is known and knowable. The Absolute cannot be known; we cannot know the Father, only the Son.[7]

> He (Christ) had no other occupation in life; no other thought except that one, that he was a Spirit. He was a disembodied, unfettered, unbound spirit. And not only so, but he, with his marvelous vision, had found that every man and woman, whether Jew or Greek, whether rich or poor, whether saint or sinner, was the embodiment of the same undying Spirit as himself. Therefore the one work his whole life showed, was calling upon them to realize their own spiritual nature . . . You are all sons of God, Immortal spirit. "Know" he declared, "the kingdom of Heaven is within you. I and my Father are one."[8]

Christ can therefore be called a yogi and a *jivanmukta;* that is, someone who has realized ultimate liberation already in this life. That is why he is a model of renunciation—a true *sannyasin.* Vivekananda maintained that Christ was basically an Oriental in spirit and that Orientals can understand and follow him better and more easily than Westerners.

Jesus, the *Satyagrahi*

Mahatma Gandhi (1869–1948) was not only a politician who led India to its independence from colonialism. He was also a deeply religious person. Though he was a Hindu and found his inspiration in the *Bhagavad Gita*, Gandhi had evolved a personal religion. For him, truth is God. The Sanskrit word for truth, *Sat,* also means "being." This truth can be realized only progressively by being faithful to the limited truths of daily life. The way of achieving this truth is *ahimsa* or nonviolence. One must be able to love the meanest creation as oneself. Non-violence is not possible without *brahmacarya*, namely, self-control and renunciation. Gandhi's personal religion, therefore, had a strongly ethical character. It is from this vantage point that he looks at all the religions, including Christianity.

For Gandhi all religions are true but imperfect. All of them show the way to God.

> I believe that all the great religions of the world are true, more or less. I say "more or less" because I believe that everything that the human hand touches, by reason of the very fact that human beings are imperfect, becomes imperfect.[9]

Given his ethical orientation and his interest in nonviolence, what attracted him in Jesus was his teaching in the Sermon on the Mount and his experience on the cross. He says: "The message of Jesus as I understand it, is contained in His Sermon on the Mount."[10] He saw in Jesus "a martyr, an embodiment of sacrifice." The cross was the symbol of this self-sacrificing love of Christ.

> The gentle figure of Christ, so patient, so kind, so loving, so full of forgiveness that he taught his followers not to retaliate when abused or struck but to turn the other cheek—it was a beautiful example, I thought, of the perfect man.[11]

> Though I cannot claim to be a Christian in the sectarian sense, the example of Jesus' suffering is a factor in the composition of my underlying faith in non-violence, which rules all my actions, worldly and temporal. Jesus lived and died in vain if he did not teach us to regulate the whole of life by the eternal Law of Love.[12]

The cross and the Sermon on the Mount thus become symbols of a way of life. Gandhi finds them valid always and everywhere in such a way that the historicity of Christ is not important to him. "I should not care if it was proved by someone that the man called Jesus never lived . . . for the Sermon on the Mount would still be true to me."[13]

> God did not bear the Cross only nineteen hundred years ago, but He bears it today, and He dies and is resurrected from day to day. It would be poor comfort to the world, if it had to depend upon a historical God who died two thousand years ago. Do not then preach the God of history but show Him as He lives today through you . . . Living Christ means a living Cross, without it life is a living death.[14]

> Joy comes, not by the infliction of pain on others, but of pain voluntarily borne by oneself.[15]

Looking at Christ as a symbol and uninterested in his historicity, Gandhi could not accept the uniqueness of Christ as the Son of God:

> It was more than I could believe that Jesus was the only incarnate Son of God . . . If God could have sons, all of us were his sons . . . God alone is absolutely perfect. When he descends to earth, He of his own accord limits himself. Jesus died on the Cross because he was limited by the flesh.[16]

Gandhi's mature tribute to Jesus reads as follows:

> I refuse to believe that there now exists or has ever existed a person that has not made use of his example to lessen his sins . . . The lives of all have, in some greater or lesser degree, been changed by his presence, his actions, and the words spoken by his divine voice . . . He belongs not solely to Christianity but to the entire world, to all races and peoples even though the doctrines they hold and the forms of worship they practice might be different from each other.[17]

Jesus, the *Advaitin*

S. Radhakrishnan, a professor of philosophy, also served as the president of India. He was not a religious figure like Gandhi or Vivekananda. He seems to have been hurt by the way the missionaries abused Hinduism as a superstitious religion. Therefore, he set himself the task of showing that Hinduism is the "eternal religion" *(sanatana dharma)* that lies behind all religions. In a comparative way he sought to show that similar doctrines and principles can be found in all religions. He, therefore, has no use for a language of uniqueness when speaking about Jesus Christ. Radhakrishnan has no difficulty in accepting the historical Jesus and the events of his passion and death on the cross. But, for him, they have a symbolic meaning:

> For me the person of Jesus is a historical fact. Christ is not a datum of history, but a judgment of history. Jesus' insight is expressive of a timeless spiritual fact.[18]

> Christ is born in the depths of spirit: we say that he passes through life, dies on the Cross and rises again. Those are not so much historical events which occurred once upon a time as universal processes of spiritual life, which are being continually accomplished in the souls of men.[19]

Radhakrishnan understands *avatara* in a twofold manner as indicating both the descent of the Divine and the ascent of man. Jesus will be an avatar in both senses. It is in this sense that he is an *advaitin* who has realized his nondual relationship with God.

> Jesus is the example of a man who has become God and none can say where His manhood ends and His divinity begins. Man and God are akin. "That art Thou—*Tat tvam asi.*"[20]

Jesus, Solidary with Suffering Humanity

In *Jesus in Indian Painting* Richard W. Taylor gives a list of more than ten Hindu painters who have found the image of Jesus an attractive theme.[21] These images of Jesus center mostly around two themes: the suffering Christ, and the child Jesus with the Madonna. The child is often presented with his hands in the gesture of protection *(abhaya mudra).* Here he joins a list of Hindu gods with similar gestures. The suffering Christ is seen as symbolic of human suffering. Christ is the more than human archetype of suffering humanity. Once, when painting Christ, K.C.S. Panikkar told a friend that he was not painting Christ but "agony" and "that Christ occurred to him as the appropriate subject."[22] Another artist, Nikhil Biswas, said that Jesus Christ symbolized for him the pain and agony of a suffering man, the fittest symbol of our age. "Europe in her zeal to make a god of him has overlooked the simple truth that he was essentially a human being."[23] Arup Das is even more explicit. Commenting on one of his art shows titled "Agony" (1970), he said:

There is no room for the good man on earth when he does appear amidst us. His life is cut short by the same people whom he loves. One such soul was Jesus of Nazareth. Near home we had Gandhiji . . . I chose Christ, to Gandhi, quite unconsciously in the beginning and then I realized that nobody suffered as much as He in all history. His crucifixion was transcendental and his agony unparalleled. In fact Agony is the theme of my paintings. Agony, not of Christ and Gandhi alone, but of Man, miserable man.[24]

Jesus becomes the symbol of suffering humanity. This is an aspect that the Hindu artists do not see in their own gods and goddesses. Indian poet and art critic P. Lal has suggested that there have been three iconographic breakthroughs in history: the suffering Christ, the smiling Buddha radiating peace, and the dancing Nataraja symbolizing dynamic creativity.[25] It is significant that just as Hindu artists have taken to painting the suffering Jesus, Indian Christian artists love to portray Jesus as seated like the Buddha in meditation or like the Nataraja, dancing in creative joy.

Jesus, the Bodhisattva

The Buddhists in general see the Buddha as one who has discovered the path to liberation or *nirvana*. He points out a way that every human can follow to reach the same goal. Some later Buddhist traditions see Buddha as an avatar or divine manifestation or even as a savior who offers the grace of liberation. What is important is the practice of meditation or mindfulness and of *karuna* (compassion) toward suffering humanity. Contemporary Buddhist leaders have no difficulty in seeing Jesus as a bodhisattva—a liberated soul, who shows the way of liberation to other humans. Thich Nhat Hanh is representative.[26] In his book *Living Buddha, Living Christ* he writes:

Sitting beneath the Bodhi tree, many wonderful, holy seeds within the Buddha blossomed forth. He was human, but, at the same time, he became an expression of the highest spirit of humanity. *When we are in touch with the highest spirit in ourselves, we too are a Buddha, filled with the Holy Spirit, and we become very tolerant, very open, very deep, and very understanding.*

Jesus is the Son of God and the Son of Man. We are all, at the same time, the sons and daughters of God and the children of our parents. This means we are of the same reality as Jesus . . . Jesus is not only our Lord, but He is also our Father, our Teacher, our Brother, and our

3

Jesus, the Sage

Every community has its sage. Every culture has its tradition of wisdom. Wisdom is not the monopoly of the social and cultural elite. Poor people too have their practical wisdom. This finds expression in stories, proverbs, and parables. These communicate the collective knowledge that the community has acquired in the course of time through its own living experience. They suggest attitudes to life and to the world and ways of relating and behaving. Some people are identified in every community as repositories of such wisdom. They teach not only in words but also by example. Others approach them for advice in times of perplexity. People are supposed to become wiser as they grow older both through experience and observation.

The wisdom of the sage has a secular character about it. It is not knowledge acquired through divine revelation. Its suggested behavior is not laid down by the positive law of God. It is what anyone who is a keen observer of nature and human life can learn. It does not simply reflect how people behave. People tend to be self-centered and imperfect. So it also indicates how people as humans ought to behave. It represents the collective awareness of the people about how humans should live. It lays down basic moral principles that guide personal life and relationships among people. Wisdom is not something that one creates like literature or poetry. It is an inner wealth of which one can become aware. It inspires and guides.

Wisdom is available to everyone. Everyone can become a wise person. But, unfortunately, prejudices can cloud one's vision. Desires can influence one's judgment. Emotion can mislead intelligence. Misbehavior can blunt one's sensitivity. So wisdom is only accessible to the few who have managed to overcome such disabilities. That is why being a sage is also a sign of character. A sage may communicate his or her wisdom to disciples, but the disciples must be worthy to learn the wisdom that is taught. In any case, one's learning matures through practice.

Sages in Asia

Asian traditions have a high regard for sages. The Chinese character for sage indicates one who listens (to nature/heaven) and speaks. Confucius thought that a sage was a perfect human being who understood the way *(Tao)* of the cosmos or heaven and lived according to it, showing the way to the others. It was an ideal that everyone should aspire to. Confucius suggested that rulers should try to be sages. But he did not dare attribute this title to anyone, certainly not to himself. The definition of a sage offered by Mencius shows us why.

> The desirable is called "good." To have it in oneself is called "true." To possess it fully in oneself is called "beautiful," but to shine forth with this full possession is called great. To be great and be transformed by this greatness is called "sage"; to be sage and to transcend the understanding is called "divine." *(Analects* 7B:25)

Mencius, however, considered Confucius a sage and thought that sagehood was attainable by the humans, though it was not easy. Confucius then becomes the guide to sagehood. His writings are carefully studied and commented upon by his successors. The wisdom of Confucius promotes a perfect life in this world.

In the Indian tradition the writers of the *Upanishads*, would certainly be considered sages. Not satisfied with the sacrificial system of the Vedas, they seek to understand the nature of the humans and of the universe. They declare the oneness of the *Brahman*—the basis of the universe—and the *Atman*—the basic identity of the humans. They say that experiencing this oneness or non-duality *(advaita)* frees humans from the cycles of phenomenal existence. Achieving such a freeing experience is the goal of life. They propose various ways of striving for such liberation: the way of wisdom or insight *(jnana)* achieved through meditation and concentration; the way of devotion *(bhakti),* which consists of loving remembrance and service of God, as Lord, in God's many grace-giving manifestations in history; the way of desireless (selfless) action or action without attachment to its fruits *(nishkama karma)*, motivated solely by the need to maintain *dharma* (world order); and the way of psycho-physical discipline *(yoga)*, unifying oneself through concentration and reaching out to the field of human and cosmic energy, of which we are not usually aware. Yoga, with its exercises for physical and mental relaxation and methods of meditation leading to inner harmony and peace, has become the common property of Asian religious and secular traditions with their roots in Hinduism and Buddhism. *Chakras* or energy nodes in the body, *asanas* or bodily postures, and *pranayama* or breathing techniques are today known the world over. Side by side with these methods we also have a popular tradition of fables (the *Panchatantra*, for example) that offer basic moral guidelines for life in the world. The epics like the *Ramayana* and the *Mahabharata* are also full of stories that illustrate ethical principles.

In South India the Tamil tradition has a series of writings that offers basic rules of moral conduct for social life. The most important among them is *Tirukkural*, which describes a way of life in the world. Setting itself in the framework of the four goals of life according to the Indian tradition—righteousness *(dharma)*, wealth *(artha)*, pleasure *(kama)*, and liberation *(moksha)*—it offers detailed guidelines for the first three of the life's goals—somewhat in the manner of Confucius.

It is in this context that both the Chinese and the Indians see Jesus as a sage who shows us, by word and example, the way of living in the world so as to reach the goal(s) of life.

The Biblical Background

The image of the sage is not foreign to the Bible. There are wisdom books in the Bible: the book of Job, Proverbs, Ecclesiastes, the Song of Solomon, and Wisdom. Israel shares this tradition with other people in the Middle East. Compared to the historical books like Genesis and Exodus, and the prophets, like Isaiah, Jeremiah, and Ezekiel, the wisdom books do not refer directly to God's intervention in the life and history of God's people. They reflect rather on God's presence in the cosmos and human life and draw lessons for life from that experience. On the one hand, they tend to affirm God's sovereignty over the world as Creator whose providence prevails in spite of what we see as unexplainable happenings that baffle us. On the other hand, they also give expression to the doubts that arise in people's minds regarding the justice and power of God when they are troubled by what they feel is unmerited suffering. There are natural and human disasters that seem unreasonable. In the midst of all this they see God's wisdom operative in the world.

The Bible also tends to personify wisdom. (We have seen this in Chapter 1.) This tendency toward the personification of wisdom seems to facilitate the efforts of the New Testament writers to understand and interpret Jesus as the incarnate Wisdom and Word of the Father. Matthew has Jesus say:

"I thank you, Father, Lord of heaven and earth, because you have hidden these things from the wise and the intelligent and have revealed them to infants; yes, Father, for such was your gracious will. All things

have been handed over to me by my Father; and no one knows the
Son except the Father, and no one knows the Father except the Son
and anyone to whom the Son chooses to reveal him." (Mt 11:25–27)

The Son mediates—embodies—God's wisdom, and it is a gift not to the
intelligent but to the simple and humble people. In exploring the theme of
Jesus as incarnate Wisdom, however, the attention of the exegetes seems to
focus more on the need to show how the divine nature of Jesus comes to
be recognized through such a process of personification than to understand
how Jesus is a wise man.

People of other religions who read the story of Jesus in the gospels, not
preoccupied with the explanation and defense of dogmatic development,
focus more on the wisdom of Jesus than on Jesus as Wisdom. They see
Jesus as a sage. In looking on Jesus as a sage, I am not denying the perspectives of Jesus as Wisdom incarnate. I am simply paying attention to the
wisdom of Jesus. Theologians' soteriological concerns make them concentrate on the passion of the Jesus who died for the sins of humanity, not on
his life and teachings. In evoking the image of Jesus as the sage I am trying
understand the significance of Jesus as a teacher and a guide for our lives
in this world through his own life and preaching. I think that this image has
appealed and will widely appeal to Asians of all religions. It will be very helpful to Christians also.

Jesus as a Teacher

Jesus was recognized as a teacher during his lifetime. The Hebrew term
for teacher is *rabbi*. It becomes a title. Not only Mary Magdalene (Jn 20:16)
but even Judas (Mt 26:49) uses it. But the title was based on what he did.
Mark tells us: "He went about among the villages teaching" (Mk 6:6). A rich
young man asks him: "Teacher, what good deed must I do to have eternal
life?" (Mt 19:16), though he was unwilling to follow his advice to sell all his
possessions, give the proceeds to the poor, and then follow him. A similar
question by a lawyer provokes Jesus to narrate the parable of the Good
Samaritan, in which a Samaritan comes to the aid of a wounded person on
the road who had been ignored by a priest and a Temple official who also
had passed that way (Lk 10:25–37). Jesus teaches the people in parables.
When their meaning is not clear, because someone is not open to the message or does not reflect, he takes care to explain them to the disciples (Mt
13:11). While John provides long discourses—to Nicodemus (Jn 3), to the
Samaritan woman (Jn 4), to the crowds after the multiplication of bread
(Jn 6), to the disciples after the final supper (Jn 13—17), and so on—de-
scribing some of his symbolic actions, Matthew summarizes his teachings

thematically. The Sermon on the Mount (Mt 5—7) has certainly attracted many Asians.

Teaching with Authority

In the Jewish tradition the prophets spoke in the name of Yahweh. "Thus says Yahweh" was their usual introduction. The scribes interpreted and explained the Bible, as do our exegetes and preachers today. But Jesus was recognized as speaking on his own authority. Matthew concludes the Sermon on the Mount with the following words: "When Jesus had finished saying these things, the crowds were astounded at his teaching, for he taught them as one having authority, and not as their scribes" (Mt 7:28–29). The authority was expressed in the manner he spoke: "You have heard that it was said . . . But I say to you . . . " (Mt 5:21–22). He did not contradict the former precept but deepened it: it is not enough to refrain from murder; we should not even insult the other, and if we have offended someone, we must seek to be reconciled with that person (Mt 5:21–26).

Jesus displayed this authority also in other ways. He "entered the temple and drove out all who were selling and buying in the temple," saying that a place of prayer should not become a market (Mt 21:12). The Jewish authorities felt challenged and questioned his authority: "By what authority are you doing these things, and who gave you this authority?" (Mt 21:23). Jesus refuses to answer them. Probably he implies that he does not need any special authority to remind them that the Temple is a place for prayer, not for buying and selling. The challenge is all the sharper because it points to an abuse of authority. Such a challenge seems to have triggered the decision of the Jewish authorities to do away with him (Jn 11:45–53).

The teaching of Jesus does not give us information about heavenly realities. He does not speak about God's inner being or life. He does not describe life in heaven. He does not set up a ritual organization focused on the sacred. When he finally leaves a sign for his disciples to remember him by, it is the common gesture of sharing a meal in community, eating and drinking together in his memory. He tells us how to live and how to relate to one another and to God. He talks in the context of life in this world. He uses ordinary examples with which everyone is familiar: the lilies in the field, the sower going out to sow, the growing corn, the trees and the birds of the air that come to rest on them, the sea and those whose living depends on it, the suffering and the marginalized poor, unjust rulers, the loving and forgiving parent. That is why his teaching has universal resonance. I shall group the teachings of Jesus in a thematic way for better understanding. I do not intend to be exhaustive. My aim is to evoke the image of Jesus as a sage.

Be Authentic

Jesus suggests that people should be *authentic* in their behavior. People are capable of thinking or intending one thing and doing another. Jesus insists that we must do what we think. We must not deceive others by doing something that we do not really mean. We are what we think and intend and not always what we do. Paul was aware of the tension. "I do not understand my own actions. For I do not do what I want, but I do the very thing I hate" (Rom 7:15). Not only our actions but our intentions too should be blameless. We may easily deceive others by what we do. But we cannot deceive ourselves. We certainly cannot deceive God. The call to authenticity could be further extended by the axiom: The end does not justify the means. Not only the end but also the means must be good.

It is not enough to refrain from murdering someone. We should not even be angry with others or abuse them. We should not cause anger in others by our behavior. Jesus goes to the extent of saying that when we go to the altar of God to make an offering, if we remember that someone has a grievance against us, we should leave our gift there, go, and be reconciled with that person and then come back and make the offering. It is significant that Jesus does not ask us to forgive others who have offended us. He takes it for granted. He asks us to go and ask forgiveness from the people whom we may have offended. The onus of seeking reconciliation is on us because we are the ones who have done wrong (Mt 5:21–26).

We may refrain from an adulterous relationship but be more free with adulterous thoughts and imaginings. Pornographic magazines and "blue" films cater to a willing audience, and the Internet has made access easy and private. Jesus does not see any difference between an adulterous intention and an adulterous action. They are equally reprehensible. We may seek to excuse ourselves by saying that the "spirit is indeed willing, but the flesh is weak." Jesus is very demanding. If our eye or our hand—our body, generally—is a cause of sin, it is better to cut it off than to yield to the evil behavior that it leads us to (Mt 5:27–30). Jesus also demands loyalty in marital relationships. He does not accept easy divorce, since it may lead to adulterous promiscuity (Mt 5:31–32).

Swearing used to be a common practice when people wanted to assure others that they were speaking the truth. They called God or the saints as witnesses. Jesus believed if we speak the truth, it can stand by itself without any other support. It is better to cultivate trustful relationships so that swearing is no longer necessary. Then we will not have to protest too much. Our relationships will be transparent. We can reduce our speech to "yes" and "no" (Mt 5:33–37).

All of us wish to be at peace with others. This supposes a capacity to adjust, overlook, forgive, yield. We can always stand on our rights and insist on retaliating when we feel that some one has wronged us: an eye for an eye, and a tooth for a tooth. Someone is stupid or wicked enough to start the process. But instead of putting an end to the chain or spiral of violence, we are tempted to continue it by paying the person back in the same coin. In a social setting we may not hit back at the guilty person but at someone from his or her group. Thus an individual enmity becomes a group conflict. The process becomes endless. The spiral can be interrupted only if someone breaks the cycle by refusing to demand an eye for an eye. Jesus suggests that we can not only stop the cycle by not responding in the same coin, but we can promote reconciliation and good feeling by being generous. "If anyone strikes you on the right cheek, turn the other also" (Mt 5:39) Not to hit back when able to do so is a demonstration of strength (human, not physical), not of weakness. I recall the aphorism of the Tamil poet Tiruvalluvar: The way to punish others who have wronged us is to shame them by doing good to them.

Be Sincere

It is not uncommon to do something, not because it needs to be done or because we like to do it, but in order to impress others. The "self" wants to be in the limelight. We do not wish so much to *be* good and holy but to *be seen to be* good and holy. Goodness is no longer seen as a value in itself but as a means of bringing us appreciation and praise. Instead of helping us to grow in goodness, such acts only feed our ego and nurture our pride. Jesus evokes scenes that may be familiar to us even today. The Jews may have sounded trumpets when they distributed alms (Mt 6:1–4). Today we hear the gesture announced and praised over loudspeakers and see the flashes of still and video cameras. Every little foundation carries a plaque with the details about its benefactors.

In prayer we speak to God. We do not need to speak to God actually, since God already knows what we need. All that we have to do is to be silent and attentive with a feeling of dependence and gratefulness, knowing that God will look after our needs, as God feeds the birds and clothes the lilies of the field. What is important are interior attitudes and not external expressions. But then, we like the others to notice that we are praying. It is like political demonstrations, which sometimes turn violent. Whether the message reaches those to whom it is directed or not, it is forced on the bystanders. The feeling of having done something and the publicity for oneself may be the real needs. Maybe some of us fool ourselves into thinking that we can force the hand of God by making our prayers public and eloquent.

Instead of a silent request we use a plethora of words. We may even try to impress ourselves by our eloquence and imagine that it will impress God (Mt 6:5–8). In these kinds of ostentatious observances we give more place to the ego than to God. We are insincere. Loud and frequent prayers are less important than listening to the word of God and doing it. Jesus says: "Not everyone who says to me, 'Lord, Lord,' will enter the kingdom of heaven, but only the one who does the will of my Father in heaven" (Mt 7:21). Jesus claims a special relationship with those who do God's will, even at the risk of seeming to belittle his own family:

> While he was still speaking to the crowds, his mother and his brothers were standing outside, wanting to speak to him. Some one told him, "Look, your mother and your brothers are standing outside, wanting to speak to you." But to the one who had told him this, Jesus replied, "Who is my mother, and who are my brothers?" And pointing to his disciples, he said, "Here are my mother and my brothers! For whoever does the will of my Father in heaven is my brother and sister and mother." (Mt 12:46–50)

While others may have been shocked by this, his own mother would have understood it, because her motherhood started with such a hearing and doing the will of God. When the angel announces to her the conception of Jesus in her womb, she responds: "Here am I, the servant of the Lord; let it be with me according to your word" (Lk 1:38). When the shepherds visit the newborn Jesus and when Jesus stays back in the temple at the age of twelve and seems to rebuke his parents saying, "Did you not know that I must be in my Father's house?" Mary treasured all these things in her heart (Lk 2:19, 51).

People seek not only to deceive God by their loud and insistent prayers. They may also try to deceive others by pretending to speak to them in the name of God. We are familiar with bogus gurus who promise instant peace and happiness. Astrologers and soothsayers pretend to predict our futures and set them right, when necessary, by appropriate rituals. Jesus warns sternly: "Beware of false prophets, who come to you in sheep's clothing but inwardly are ravenous wolves. You will know them by their fruits" (Mt 7:15–16).

Fasting is a way of disciplining ourselves. Fasting can be taken to stand for ascetical practices in general. As a means of self-discipline, such practices can be useful. They train us to control our fleshly and egoistic desires. But like almsgiving and prayer they can be used to impress others. In India we know yogis who assume unusual postures, lie on a bed of nails, or get themselves buried under the ground. It is known that the body has under-utilized sources of energy that we can tap by mental and will power and appropriate physical exercises. Some may take to these practices to acquire supranormal—though not supra-human—powers and then use them to impress others. Others may use them more simplistically to gain merit, either to make reparation for sins or to gain rewards from God. Exploring the supra-normal powers of the human person is good and can help healing and wholeness. These are natural human powers, and there is no harm in becoming aware of them and using them for our life and growth. Some contemporary healing systems and alternative therapies like Reiki, touch therapy, and pranic healing, based on the principles of yoga, seek to do so. But we need not use them for self-exhibition.

Be with Others

Humans are social beings. We are born and grow in a family. We interiorize the language and culture of a group of people. Our lives are constantly dependent on a host of others, the goods they produce, and the services they offer. Our temptation is to exploit them for our own benefit. We look on others as objects to be used to build up our own ego. Social structures like feudalism and the caste system have been devised to dominate and exploit groups of people. Such hierarchy and injustice provoke conflict. People seek freedom and justice. They attempt to build community. They quest for peace and harmony. But as we have seen, following a principle of retributive justice expressed by the phrase "an eye for an eye, a tooth for a tooth" can lead only to a spiral of violence. If the process continues, everyone will end up blind and toothless. So people suggest today a principle of restorative justice, which breaks the cycle of violence and restores community. Its focus is not the individual and his or her rights only, but also the individual's duties toward the community. The community too has rights. This would involve a spirit of give and take as people learn to forgive, try to forget the past, and seek to build the future. Forgiveness and love rather than revenge and exploitation become principles of social life and organization. Jesus has laid down the foundations for this by his own life and teaching.

Jesus repeats the golden rule that can be found in many cultural traditions in varying formulations: "In everything do to others as you would have them do to you" (Mt 7:12). But he goes much beyond this. He suggests that our sense of justice may often be misguided by our prejudices and selfishness. So he warns us, "Do not judge, so that you may not be judged" (Mt 7:1). Then he adds, "Why do you see the speck in your neighbor's eye, but do not notice the log in your own eye?" (Mt 7:3). Sensitivity to our own shortcomings will make us more sensitive to the needs and attitudes of the others. That is why Jesus says, "Give to everyone who begs from you, and do not refuse anyone who wants to borrow from you" (Mt 5:42). As a matter of fact, we could be more magnanimous, so that our gift is more the measure of our generosity than the need of the other. "If anyone wants to sue you and take your coat, give your cloak as well; and if anyone forces you to go one mile, go also the second mile" (Mt 5:40–41).

Be Loving

In relating to others in this way we may not go beyond the practical demands of life together in a group. It could be a policy of live and let live. We learn to make adjustments in the process of common living. Jesus takes this one step further when he says that we must love each other. He refers back to a biblical commandment. Answering a Pharisee who asks, "Which commandment in the law is the greatest?" he says, "You shall love the Lord your God with all your heart, and with all your soul, and with all your mind. This is the greatest commandment. And a second is like it: You shall love your neighbor as yourself" (Mt 22:36–39). In his own teaching Jesus reduces this double commandment to one. He says, "I give you a new commandment, that you love one another" (Jn 13:34). The implication is that we love God in others. He actually explains this in his evocation of the scene of the judgment of the nations at the end of the world. There the Son of Man rewards good people, saying: "I was hungry and you gave me food, I was thirsty and you gave something to drink, I was a stranger and you welcomed me, I was naked and you gave me clothing, I was in prison and you visited me." The people do not recognize themselves in this description and express surprise. They ask: "When did this happen?" And the Son of Man answers: "Truly I tell you, just as you did it to one of the least of these who are members of my family, you did it to me" (Mt 25:31–40).

The stress in this relationship is not on the people who are hungry, thirsty, naked, and so forth. It is not their worthiness that is considered. What is important is our openness and readiness to help whoever is in need. It is an attitude of selflessness that reaches out to everyone and comes to the aid of those who are in need. This aspect comes out clearly in the parable of the Good Samaritan (Lk 10:25–37). There is the robbed and wounded man beside the road. The priest and the Temple official pass him by. They may have thought only of their convenience, their urgency to reach the Temple, and their ritual purity. We do not know. But the Samaritan thinks only of the needs of the wounded man. He cares for him, takes him to an inn, and provides for his continuing care till he is healed. What is important here is not the worthiness or the lovableness of the individual in need. The focus is on the one who helps, whose heart is selfless and open. To love is to have such an open heart. It goes out spontaneously to others irrespective of their caste,

race, creed, sex, family, or friendship ties. Its involvement and action are
triggered when the other is in need. Love becomes active where and when
it is needed. In the parable of the Good Samaritan, to the Pharisee's question "Who is my neighbor?" Jesus does not say that the wounded man on
the road is his neighbor; rather, he says that the Samaritan was a true neighbor to the wounded man. Our neighborliness is determined by love that is
open always, everywhere and to everyone, not by the identity and/or worthiness of the other. We do not look for suitable neighbors to love. We are
neighborly to everyone. Love, therefore, is not a mere emotion. It has to be
shown in action. Jesus indicates that the selflessness of love can be total. He
tells the disciples at the very moment when disaster for himself seems to be
looming large in the horizon, "No one has greater love than this, to lay down
one's life for one's friends" (Jn 15:13). Other texts in the New Testament
illustrate this one, for example, "God so loved the world that he gave his only
Son" (Jn 3:16). Jesus continues: "Just as the living Father sent me, and I live
because of the Father, so whoever eats me will live because of me" (Jn 6:57).
The reference to eating may sound cannibalistic till we realize that it refers
to oneness in life and that the whole operation is done symbolically through
bread and wine (Mt 26:26–29). Communion in life is made possible through
sharing and self-gift—giving not only what one has, but what one is.

Jesus makes himself present bodily in the very act in which a group of
people share food and drink together. At the final supper with his disciples
Jesus breaks bread, gives it to them, and says, "Take, eat, this is my body."
Then he takes a cup of wine, gives it to them saying, "Drink from it all of
you; for this is my blood of the covenant" (Mt 26:26–28). In the very act of
sharing, the bread and the wine become the body and blood of Jesus. That
is to say, Jesus becomes bodily present in the meal. Sharing food and drink
is a symbol of sharing one's life, which the food nourishes. Sharing one's
possessions is only an external symbol of this sharing of life. The early community of Christians realized this. We are told:

> All who believed were together and had all things in common; they
> would sell their possessions and goods and distribute the proceeds to
> all, as any had need. Day by day, as they spent much time together in
> the temple, they broke bread at home and ate their food with glad and
> generous hearts, praising God and having the goodwill of all the
> people. (Acts 2:44–47)

Another manifestation of such mutual love is service. We saw this in the
parable of the Good Samaritan. In this parable the focus is on the Samaritan, who is open to helping anyone in need without asking questions. Such
readiness to give what one is and what one has supposes humility and

egolessness. Jesus illustrates this by washing the feet of his disciples (Jn 13:1–11). He tells his disciples after that:

> "Do you know what I have done to you? You call me Teacher and Lord—and you are right, for that is what I am. So if I, your Lord and Teacher, have washed your feet, you also ought to wash one another's feet. For I have set you an example, that you also should do as I have done to you." (Jn 13:12–15)

Jesus had told them earlier: "Learn from me, for I am gentle and humble in heart" (Mt 11:29). Here he shows what such humility means in practice. The process of thought is simple: to be a community is to love one another; to love is to give; to give is to be egoless; to be egoless is to be humble; to be humble is to serve. This is how humans are expected to be. Selfishness, pride, and hatred of others are not human. More than harming others they hurt one's own self. They make us dissatisfied and unhappy, tense, and angry. They consume us from within like a cancer. They depress us. They can make us physically sick. Loving the others is good for us and for our psychological and physical health and wholeness. That is why Jesus goes one step further.

It is easy to love those who love us. We can manage to love those who are related to us in some way. Having a heart open to everyone is more difficult, though we know that there are people who do that. But we may like to draw a line before people who are opposed to us in some way. We see them as enemies who do not wish our good. So we can understand the injunction to "love your neighbor and hate your enemy" (Mt 5:43). But Jesus says, with authority, "But I say to you, Love your enemies and pray for those who persecute you" (Mt 5:44). He goes on to give a reason:

> ". . . so that you may be children of your Father in heaven; for he makes his sun rise on the evil and on the good, and sends rain on the righteous and on the unrighteous. For if you love those who love you, what reward do you have? Do not even the tax collectors do the same? And if you greet only your brothers and sisters, what more are you doing than others? Do not even the Gentiles do the same? Be perfect, therefore, as your heavenly Father is perfect." (Mt 5:45–48)

This reference to the heavenly Father may make this appear an impossible ideal, more a source of inspiration than a norm for behavior. But Jesus does not seem to propose this as something superhuman. It is possible for the humans, precisely because we are children of this Father. Love of enemies starts with forgiveness. It is significant that where Matthew says "be perfect as your heavenly Father is perfect," Luke has "be merciful, just as your Father is merciful" (Lk 6:36). Perfection is related to being merciful and forgiving. That is why forgiveness seems to be one of the major messages of the life and teaching of Jesus.

Be Forgiving

Jesus also links forgiveness to love. We are familiar with the story of the sinful woman who comes to Jesus when he is the guest of a Pharisee and, to the astonishment of all, weeps, bathes the feet of Jesus with her tears, and wipes them with her hair. She then anoints his feet with perfume and kisses them (Lk 7:36–38). After a brief conversation with the Pharisee, Jesus tells him: "I tell you, her sins, which were many, have been forgiven; hence she has shown great love" (Lk 7:47). We see a link between love and forgiveness, but also a reversal of perspectives. Jesus does not say, "She has loved, and therefore she is forgiven." He says, "She has been forgiven, and therefore she loves." We can discern a process here: Forgiveness is certainly preceded by an acknowledgment of guilt and repentance. They represent an incipient love, though it goes together with a sense of unworthiness. In the presence of Jesus the woman realizes that she has been forgiven and so responds with her gestures of love. Jesus calls her basic attitude faith. He tells the woman, "Your faith has saved you; go in peace" (Lk 7:50).

Jesus also links forgiveness to healing. Impressed by the faith of those who bring a paralytic to him and lower him through the roof because it is too crowded to get through the door, Jesus says: "Friend, yours sins are forgiven you . . . I say to you, stand up and take your bed and go to your home" (Lk 5:20, 24).

We know the story of the prodigal son: the love of the father forgives and welcomes back the wayward son. The younger son gets his half of the property, spends it in riotous living, and ends up feeding pigs for survival. He then repents and turns back. The waiting father embraces him and rehabilitates him in the household, much to the displeasure of the elder brother (Lk 15:11–24). God does not even wait for the sinners to come back but goes looking for them, as the shepherd who goes after the lost sheep, leaving the ninety-nine others, or the woman who searches for the lost coin with light and a broom (Lk 15:3–10). During his own life he befriends the tax collectors and the sinners rather than the self-righteous Pharisees (Lk 15:1–2).

Jesus also offers us his own example. Hanging on the cross, he prays for those who are crucifying him: "Father, forgive them; for they do not know what they are doing" (Lk 23:34).

God's practice of forgiving is an example for us to forgive others. But Jesus also links our forgiving others to God's forgiving us. He narrates the parable of a servant who is forgiven his debts by his master but refuses to forgive his own debtors; the master then takes him to task and punishes him. Jesus then draws the lesson: "So my heavenly Father will also do to every one of you, if you do not forgive your brother or sister from your heart" (Mt 18:35). He integrates this into the prayer that he teaches his disciples:

> "And forgive us our debts,
>   as we also have forgiven our debtors." (Mt 6:12)

He does not want them to set any limits to this forgiveness either. When Peter thinks that to forgive an offending brother seven times is praiseworthy, Jesus responds: "Not seven times, but, I tell you, seventy-seven times" (Mt 18:22). This is equivalent to always. Forgiveness, therefore, is one way that love can find expression in a practical manner.

Be Discerning

Loving and forgiving can be expressed in terms of a community comprised of people who want to live together. They prevent them from slipping into a spiral of violence. But they require selflessness. This is neither normal nor easy. So God comes into the picture as an example. With the coming of God, however, human life acquires another dimension. God is not merely our model and inspiration. God also energizes us. At the same time there are forces that pull us in the opposite direction. The New Testament names them Satan and Mammon. Mammon is the power of money. Jesus says very clearly: "No one can serve two masters . . . You cannot serve God and wealth" (Mt 6:24). The rich young man who expresses a wish to be perfect offers us a concrete example. Jesus tells him to go and sell his possessions and then to come and follow him. But the rich young man goes away grieving, "for he had many possessions" (Mt 19:22). This leads Jesus to say, "It is easier for a camel to go through the eye of a needle than for someone who is rich to enter the kingdom of God" (Mt 19:24). Money is not desired for its own sake, but for the comforts and influence that it can buy. Money is a way to social and political power. It feeds one's egotism. People who are after money do not hesitate to exploit and oppress others. At the time of Jesus, the poor were multiply exploited, paying taxes to the Romans and to the Jewish leaders and abused by the tax collectors who were their agents. Jesus condemns such slavery to money:

> "But woe to you who are rich,
>   for you have received your consolation." (Lk 6:24)

We have to choose between God and money.

Satan is the personal principle of evil that sets one against God. It expresses itself through egotism and pride. It hinders us from doing God's will. Jesus himself was tempted by Satan all through his life (Lk 4:13). At the very beginning of his public life Jesus is tempted to use the powers given to him by God for his own benefit. He is tempted to feed his hunger by turning stone into bread. He is promised power over the whole world, provided he submits to Satan rather than to God. Finally, he is asked to tempt God by throwing himself down from the top of the Temple, hoping that God's angels will support him (Lk 4:1–12). During his public life people ask him for special signs (Mt 12:38). When Jesus foretells his coming suffering, Peter remonstrates with him saying, "This must never happen to you" (Mt 16:22). Peter is rebuked by Jesus: "Get behind me, Satan! You are a stumbling block to me; for you are setting your mind not on divine things but on human things" (Mt 16:23). Even when he is hanging on the cross, he is challenged, "If you are the Son of God, come down from the cross" (Mt 27:40).

Every human is subject to the temptations of Satan and Mammon. Jesus advises his disciples, "Stay awake and pray that you may not come into the time of trial; the spirit indeed is willing, but the flesh is weak" (Mt 26:41). He also teaches them to pray to the Father:

> "And do not bring us to the time of trial,
>   but rescue us from the evil one." (Mt 6:13)

Be Ready to Choose

This contrast between God and Satan-Mammon points to contrasting ways of life in the world. People in the world want to be self-sufficient. They want to amass wealth. They wish to be honored. They like to dominate and exploit others. They tend to treat people like objects and use them for their own benefit. Jesus, however, tells them that this is not success. He lists those who are really successful:

> "Blessed are the poor in spirit,
>   for theirs in the kingdom of heaven.
> Blessed are those who mourn,
>   for they will be comforted.
> Blessed are the meek,
>   for they will inherit the earth.
> Blessed are those who hunger and thirst for
>   righteousness,
>   for they will be filled.

Blessed are the merciful,
    for they will receive mercy.
Blessed are the pure in heart,
    for they will see God.
Blessed are the peacemakers,
    for they will be called the children of God.
Blessed are those who are persecuted for righteousness'
      sake,
    for theirs is the kingdom of heaven." (Mt 5:3–10)

Here we see a contrast between the people who are poor, meek, merciful, mourning, hungering after righteousness, pure of heart, peacemakers, and persecuted, and others who are rich, proud, and so on. The latter are the ones who seem to be successful in the world. They count success in terms of wealth, power, violence, and domination. They love to subjugate others. But those who trust in God and live by God's values may not succeed in the world in these terms. They will remain poor, and they will suffer. The question is who is really happy: the rich, with their limitless ambition that never says enough, or the poor, who find true love and fellowship even in their poverty. We should not commit the mistake of saying that the poor who suffer now will be rewarded in a future life. Without denying such future happiness, already in this life the poor enjoy love of and fellowship with one another. There is a deep sense of satisfaction that underlies even poverty, while it escapes the rich. I think this is what Jesus asserts symbolically when he tells Peter, "Truly I tell you, there is no one who has left house or wife or brothers or parents or children, for the sake of the kingdom of God, who will not get back very much more in this age, and in the age to come eternal life" (Lk 18:29–30). The distinction that Jesus makes between this age and the age to come is worth noting.

So Jesus speaks of two worlds, not this world and the next, but the world of humans and the world of God. The world of God overlaps and transcends the world of humans. It is more real. The contrast is really between depending on oneself and depending on God. There are people whose life is oriented to achievement. They want to be self-made people. They pursue success. There are others who do everything as they should but at the same time leave everything to God. They are dependent on God. Jesus gives the example of the birds of the air and the lilies of the field. God will look after us as God looks after them. After all, we are more precious to God. We need not worry about the things of this world. God will provide (Mt 6:25–32). Jesus concludes, "Strive first for the kingdom of God and his righteousness, and all these things will be given to you as well" (Mt 6:33).

Jesus plays constantly on this contrast. There is the rich fool who has a good harvest, stores it in his barns, and dreams of a happy life without knowing that he is going to die that night (Lk 12:16–21). He depends on himself and his achievements. Jesus also contrasts storing up treasures on the earth and in heaven, adding "where your treasure is, there your heart will be also" (Mt 6:19–21). It is no wonder that people who represent these two tendencies do not get along well in this world. People who believe in this world and in themselves want to be dominant, and they do not hesitate to oppress and exploit the others. So the latter are persecuted. But the persecutors can kill only the body, not the soul. So we need not be afraid of them. We are actually concerned, not with a different world, but with a different *dimension* of the world. The contrast is between a world that is centered on money and power and another that is based on love and service. Both worlds can coexist in the same geographical and social space. But they do not really compete with each other on the same level.

When Jesus is standing before Pilate, he asks Jesus, "Are you the King of the Jews?" Jesus assures him: "My kingdom is not from this world" (Jn 18:33, 36). By the term *world* here Jesus is referring to the kind of situation in which Pilate is operating. Jesus is not competing for space and power in that world. But there is another world of which Jesus speaks:

> Pilate asked him again, "So you are a king?" Jesus answered, "You say that I am a king. For this I was born, and for this I came into the world, to testify to the truth. Everyone who belongs to the truth listens to my voice." (Jn 18:37)

These two worlds—the world of Pilate and the world of Jesus—do not come one after the other in time or space. They coexist in the same historical/geographical world. It is for each one of us to decide in which world we want to live.

Contrast and Paradox

It is in the context of this contrast that we have to understand the paradoxical sayings of Jesus:

> "Do not think that I have come to bring peace to the earth; I have not come to bring peace, but a sword.
>   For I have come to set a man against his father,
>   and a daughter against her mother,
>   and a daughter-in-law against her mother-in-law;
>   and one's foes will be members of one's own household.

Whoever loves father or mother more than me is not worthy of me; and whoever loves son or daughter more than me is not worthy of me; and whoever does not take up the cross and follow me is not worthy of me. Those who find their life will lose it, and those who lose their life for my sake will find it." (Mt 10:34–39)

In the context of the struggle between the ego and God, between the ego's relationships and plans and God's relationships and plans, values like peace and life acquire a double meaning and realization. It is in this same context that we have to understand: "The last will be first, and the first will be last" (Mt 20:16). The last in one world will be the first in the other. These are not two worlds in temporal succession. They are two ways of living, two communities with two different world views, attitudes, and systems of values.

Be in the Present

The choice between life and death, between God and Mammon/Satan, is a constant one. Jesus presents this as a response to the call of God to the kingdom: "The time is fulfilled, and the kingdom of God has come near; repent and believe in the good news" (Mk 1:15). This kingdom is not to be realized with a big bang in the near or the distant future. On the contrary, it is like a seed that has been sown and is constantly growing here and now in unknown ways (Mk 4:3–9, 26–32). It is like leaven that is working within without being noticed (Mt 13:33). Every moment, therefore, is a time for decision. To be converted or to turn to God in this situation is to do as God does: to love and serve the other, giving oneself even unto death. It does not consist in observing elaborate legal and ritual prescriptions. We can put it simply by saying that we are called to be authentically and sincerely human, not "religious" in an institutional or ritual sense. The demands of Jesus are applicable and can be met by all people of whatever religion. All can love and forgive. Everyone can serve others in need.

Sabbath or the Human

In his own life Jesus opposes the Pharisees who observe strictly legal prescriptions of purity and pollution and ritual obligations like the sabbath as ways of pleasing God. They are faithful to various ablutions and washing their hands before meals. They would not sit at table with people whom they consider ritually polluted, like tax collectors and prostitutes and the poor, who do not strictly observe all the legal prescriptions as they themselves do. Jesus challenges them by healing people on the sabbath and declaring that the

sabbath is for people, not people for the sabbath (Mt 12:1–14; Lk 13:10–
17). He does not keep their laws of purity and pollution, and he eats with
the marginalized tax collectors and sinners. He tells the protesting Pharisees:
"Go and learn what this means, 'I desire mercy, not sacrifice'" (Mt 9:13). He
shocks his host, who was a Pharisee, by allowing himself to be touched by
a sinful woman (Lk 7:39). When the leaders—the scribes and the Pharisees—
want to stone a woman taken in adultery, he calls their bluff, saying, "Let
anyone among you who is without sin be the first to throw a stone at her"
(Jn 8:7). All of them slyly sneak away. He defies their social discrimination
by openly visiting the house of Matthew (Mt 9:9–10) and Zacchaeus (Lk
19:1–10), who were tax collectors. He not only fraternizes with non-Jews,
like the Samaritan (Jn 4:7–42) and the Canaanite woman (Mt 15:21–28),
but openly extols their faith. He justifies his behavior by telling the crowds,
"It is not what goes into the mouth that defiles a person, but it is what comes
out of the mouth that defiles" (Mt 15:11). Then he explains:

> "Do you not see that whatever goes into the mouth enters the stom-
> ach and goes out into the sewer? But what comes out of the mouth
> proceeds from the heart, and this is what defiles. For out of the heart
> come evil intentions, murder, adultery, fornication, theft, false witness,
> slander. These are what defile a person, but to eat with unwashed
> hands does not defile." (Mt 15:17–20)

Thus he transgresses the social and ritual/religious taboos set up by the
Pharisees and upholds the dignity of being human.

The Mystery of Unjust Suffering

It is the tension between the two kinds of people in the world in the context of God's ultimate providence that explains unjust suffering in the world.
We tend to believe simplistically that good people should be rewarded and
evil ones punished. But in our experience this is not what happens. It is the
good and the just who seem to suffer. The life and sufferings of Jesus offer
a solution to this problem.

There are many kinds of sufferings in the world. Among them we can
discount natural catastrophes like earthquakes, floods, and tsunamis as inevitable in an evolving world. Similarly, we can also see many illnesses as part
of the natural process, though we may bring some of these on ourselves by
our own unhealthy habits. But there is always a residue of suffering imposed
unjustly on us by others, especially when we are struggling for justice. We
have to be loyal to the cause of justice even unto death. We not only hope

but are sure that God will not abandon us. When we are struggling for justice, there is an inner peace and satisfaction that does not deny but transcends suffering. It is like a woman suffering the pangs of childbirth. The joy of creation is hidden in it. Heroes who sacrifice their life for their country do not provoke our commiseration but admiration. They themselves experience the suffering differently, as a challenge. They welcome it. They foresee the success that it will bring.

This is the message and example of the struggle, death, and resurrection of Jesus. Jesus is quite aware of the fact that he will have to suffer. He foresees the pain but does not flinch from it. He says:

> "Blessed are you when people revile you and persecute you and utter all kinds of evil against you falsely on my account. Rejoice and be glad, for your reward is great in heaven, for in the same way they persecuted the prophets who were before you." (Mt 5:11–12)

Jesus was conscious that death was the destiny of all the prophets (Mt 23:34). He had the example of John the Baptist, who was beheaded because he condemned the adulterous relationship of Herod with his brother's wife (Mt 14:1–12). He warns the disciples of the coming persecution. "See, I am sending you out like sheep into the midst of wolves . . . They will hand you over to councils and flog you in their synagogues . . . You will be hated by all because of my name" (Mt 10:16, 17, 22). But he was sure that the final victory will be God's (Mt 16:21; 17:9). The apostles learned the lesson. When they were flogged by the Jewish leaders, "they rejoiced that they were considered worthy to suffer dishonor for the sake of the name" (Acts 5:41).

This was the deepest element in the wisdom of Jesus. Given the kind of world in which we are living, the suffering of the just is inevitable. But suffering and death will not be the last word. Life will continue. It is not the kind of life that people normally live in the world. At the same time, it is not simply a life after death, after history. It is a different kind of life in and with God that can already be lived here and now. The Bible often opposes earth to heaven. These should not be seen as two different kinds of world. Our popular cosmology sees heaven as another world coming after death. This may be a wrong perception. When Jesus tells the Jews after multiplying bread for them, "I am the living bread that came down from heaven. Whoever eats of this bread will live forever; and the bread that I will give for the life of the world is my flesh" (Jn 6:51), he is speaking of a life that we can share with God here and now, not only after death. This life will not die or disappear. This life is contemporaneous with the ordinary life in the world. The "living water" that Jesus promises the Samaritan woman has the same significance (Jn 4:14).

Similarly, Paul assures us that in baptism we die with Christ and rise with him into newness of life. This new life has to be lived here and now (Rom 6:1–14). Paul would contrast these two lives—two worlds—as life according to the flesh and to the Spirit (see Gal 5:16–26) or old and new life (Eph 4:17—5:2; Col 3). He lists the fruits of the Spirit: "love, joy, peace, patience, kindness, generosity, faithfulness, gentleness, and self-control" (Gal 5:22–23).

The problem of suffering is the central problem in religious reflection. The idea that suffering is a punishment for sin is quite widespread. When they meet a man born blind, even the disciples ask Jesus, "'Rabbi, who sinned, this man or his parents, that he was born blind?' Jesus answered, 'Neither this man nor his parents sinned; he was born blind so that God's works may be revealed in him'" (Jn 9:2–3). Hinduism has the doctrine of *karma*, which says that every action will have its reward or punishment, in this life or in the next. According to the *Bhagavad Gita,* we can escape this cycle with the grace of God only if we succeed in totally detaching ourselves from the fruits of the action *(nishkama karma).* Buddhism recommends an accepting detachment. I suffer, but I try to stand mentally apart from it, taking it as an impermanent phenomenon, so that I am not personally affected by it. I take it as a matter of course. In the Old Testament we have two sorts of attempts. Job suffers and protests that he does not deserve to suffer because he has been a just man. But God does not offer any justification. At the end, Job can only bow down to God's unfathomable mystery and freedom (Jb 42:1–6). The book of Wisdom is sure that just people, though they suffer at the hands of the wicked in this world, will be rewarded by God (Wis 5).

Jesus gets out of this framework linking sin and suffering, punishment and reward. He rejects the idea that suffering is a punishment for sin, as we saw in his response to the disciples concerning the man born blind. Unjust suffering may still be imposed by the wicked on the good. But the just embrace it as an expression of their struggle against injustice. So it becomes a symbol of their love and loyalty. We do not run away from suffering but accept it and give it a new meaning. God raises Jesus, giving him new life, according to our phenomenal perception. It is not a reward for his suffering. It is an expression, a manifestation of a life with God that he never actually loses. It is precisely because of this communion of life with God that he has to suffer at the hands of people who reject God in their own favor. Jesus says, "Just as the living Father sent me, and I live because of the Father, so whoever eats me will live because of me" (Jn 6:57). Jesus never loses this life. This life transforms his human life. But through the struggle and the suffering, Jesus is slowly transforming this world, changing peoples' attitudes and relationships. In this way God will eventually set the whole thing right, "so that God's work will be revealed" (Jn 9:3). Suffering becomes a symbol—

4

Jesus,
the Way

When we think of symbols for Jesus, a common one that comes to mind is that of the way. Of course, Jesus uses it of himself: "I am the way, and the truth, and the life" (Jn 14:6). The setting in which Jesus says this is significant. He is talking to his disciples after washing their feet and sharing a meal with them, offering his own body and blood in the symbols of bread and wine as food and drink. He indicates to them that he will be leaving them soon. He speaks of the impending betrayal by one of his own disciples and of the coming suffering, though he would not have known it in all its actual detail. The disciples who have been following him faithfully for some time are upset. Peter asks him: "Lord, where are you going?" and declares: "I will lay down my life for you." He has sensed the possible dangers ahead. Jesus quietly tells Peter that in a few hours' time Peter will deny any knowledge of him. Jesus says again that he is only going ahead to prepare a place for them and will come again to take them with him and adds, "And you know the way to the place where I am going." Then Thomas comes in: "Lord, we do not know where you are going. How can we know the way?" (Jn 13:31-38; 14:5). Jesus responds:

> "I am the way, and the truth, and the life. No one comes to the Father except through me. If you know me, you will know my Father also. From now on you know him and have seen him." Philip said to him, "Lord, show us the Father and we will be satisfied." Jesus said to him, "Have I been with you all this time, Philip, and you still do not know me? Whoever has seen me has seen the Father. How can you say, 'Show us the Father'? Do you not believe that I am in the Father and the Father is in me? The words that I say to you I do not speak on my own; but the Father who dwells in me does his works. Believe me that I am in the Father and the Father in me; but if you do not, then believe me because of the works themselves.

"Very truly, I tell you, the one who believes in me will also do the works that I do and, in fact, will do greater works than these, because I am going to the Father. I will do whatever you ask in my name, so that the Father may be glorified in the Son. If in my name you ask me for anything, I will do it." (Jn 14:6-14)

Jesus then goes on to promise the gift of the Spirit, who will make these promises real. A simple reading of this passage show how complex these images are. Jesus says that he is going to the Father. He is also the way to the Father. He speaks the words of the Father and does the Father's works. Their union is so intimate that he speaks of mutual indwelling. There is even a tone of identity when he says that those who see him see the Father. It is even more surprising that this relationship is extended to the disciples, who will do his, and therefore his Father's, works. The relationship, however, does not exclude a differentiation since they have to ask Jesus and, in his name, the Father to accomplish what they do. Jesus too is subject to this differentiation since he goes on to say that he will ask the Father, who will give them the Spirit (see Jn 14:16).

Theologians can wrestle with whether this relationship is operational or functional or of mutual indwelling or identity. Perhaps one does not have to choose. It is a relationship or union that can manifest itself in a variety of ways under different circumstances. Seeking to contain it in a category may not be helpful. It is a dynamic relationship with various aspects. We have to explore its richness without trying to reduce it to one of its aspects in order to make it conform to our own metaphysical presuppositions. To call Jesus the way evokes not only multipolar and multilevel relationships but also a dynamic process. To walk along that way is to be involved in these relationships.

Christianity itself was known as the Way, according to the Acts of the Apostles. Saul, who became Paul later, obtained the recommendation of the high priest to go to Damascus and arrest any one "who belonged to the Way" (Acts 9:2).

The Way in China

The symbol of the way evokes rich resonances in Asia. In the Chinese religio-cultural tradition one would think immediately of the *Tao,* and in the Indian religious tradition one would recall the *marga.* Buddha also spoke of the eightfold path. A look at these would enrich our own understanding of the richness of the symbol of the way.

The term *Tao* is used both in the Taoist and Confucian traditions in China, but in different ways. I will not discuss the internal disputes among various schools here, but rather will try to present a general sense that will be helpful for us to understand Jesus as the way and his specificity. For the Taoists, the *Tao* is nature or reality that is alive, dynamic, and in movement. It is constituted by the interplay of the active principle *yang* and the receptive-generative principle *yin*. This interplay is manifested in the different forces of nature: the sun and the moon, the winds and the rivers, the living beings and their activities. It leads to harmony. The interplay may sometimes seem confrontational: earthquakes, deluges, tsunamis. But they too are part of nature's flow or harmony. This is the *tao*. Everything in nature, including humans, is meant to live according to the flow of nature. Humans bring pain and destruction on themselves and on nature by deviating from the *tao*. The remedy is to seek to live in accordance with the flow of nature, the *tao*. They will then find peace and harmony in themselves, with others, and with the universe. The source of the problems in the universe is aggressive interference with the flow of nature by humans. The taoist ideal is to avoid this kind of aggressive action. So it speaks of non-action *(wu-wei)*. This does not mean doing nothing, but rather refraining from action that interferes with the natural flow or movement. The *Tao-Te Ching* describes non-action thus:

> The sage manages affairs without action *(wu-wei)*
> And spreads doctrines without words.
> All things arise, and he does not turn away from them.
> He produces them, but does not take possession of them.
> He acts, but does not rely on his own ability.
> He accomplishes his task, but does not claim credit for it.
> It is precisely because he does not claim credit that his
>   accomplishment remains with him.
> (*Tao-Te Ching*, 2)

The sage does not force anything, knowing that violence will only provoke more violence and start a spiral of violence. This does not mean that the sage does nothing. A sage's action is quiet and persistent, overcoming the opponent by using his or her own force, as do some of the Japanese martial arts like judo. It is like swimming along with the current. Indeed, *Tao* can be compared to water:

> There is nothing softer and weaker than water,
> And yet there is nothing better for attacking hard and
>   strong things.
> For this reason there is no substitute for it.
> All the world knows that the weak overcomes the strong
>   and the soft overcomes the hard. (*Tao-Te Ching*, 78)

Tao is the female force that stoops to conquer. It is not aggressive. But it is not passive. It is receptive and generative. That is why

> To yield is to be preserved whole.
> To be bent is to become straight.
> To be empty is to be full. (*Tao-Te Ching*, 22)

Only emptiness can be filled. The *Tao-Te Ching* illustrates this beautifully.

> Thirty spokes are united around the hub to make a
>   wheel,
>   but it is on its non-being that the utility of the carriage
>   depends.
> Clay is molded to form a utensil,
>   but it is on its non-being that the utility of the utensil
>   depends.
> Doors and windows are cut out to make a room,
>   but it is on its non-being that the utility of the room
>   depends. (*Tao-Te Ching*, 11)

The Confucian tradition would basically agree with this vision of Taoism as a framework. But it is very sensitive to the fact that humans are free and do not follow nature's way. Their self-centered behavior upsets the natural order. The natural harmony is broken. People can interfere even with natural processes through science and technology. Individuals can choose to withdraw from this actual world and seek to live in conformity with nature. They may achieve personal harmony and harmony with nature in an ideal world that they have created. But their action will not restore social and cosmic harmony. A socially responsible person, therefore, will have to work to restore social and cosmic harmony. This is done through proper relationships and appropriate ritual. Confucius spells out five kinds of basic relationships: between the king and his subjects, between the old and the young, between parents and children, between husband and wife, and between friends. The ritual order specifies the way one relates to the others from one's own situation and position in the community. But the rituals only spell out the way of Nature (or Heaven). The way of Nature is no longer natural but has to be reconstructed in a world fragmented by self-centered human behavior. In social ritual the *Tao* acquires a political dimension. While a Confucian will look on the Taoist as a passive idealist, the Taoist will look on the Confucian as an aggressive busybody seeking to interfere with the way of Nature.

In a broader perspective we can say that the Taoist and the Confucian represent the *yin* and the *yang* elements in the community. While Confucians insist that corrective action needs to be taken in the world as it is, they would agree with Taoists that the ultimate norm of behavior is the *Tao* of Nature or Heaven. The *tao,* however, is not static, but in movement, dynamic, with the ongoing interaction between the *yin* and the *yang*.

The way or *Tao* in Chinese tradition therefore represents the way reality or nature is. Humans do not always conform to this *way*. Their freedom and egotism make them stray from the way. So they have to come back to it and conform to it. This coming back does not mean relapsing into passivity, doing nothing, letting nature takes its course as material things or animals do, but, as free beings, behaving as one ought to behave, acting creatively but non-aggressively, being constantly in touch with their deeper self.

The Way in India

India is a cradle of many religions. Besides Hinduism, it has given birth to Jainism, Buddhism, and Sikhism. Underlying all these is a religio-cultural tradition of praxis or *sadhana*. Though elements of it are also found in other religions, this is perhaps spelled out most clearly in Hinduism. So I shall focus on Hinduism. It speaks of four ways or *margas* of reaching liberation. They are *jnana* (insight or wisdom), *bhakti* (love or devotion), *karma* (ritual or moral action), and *yoga* (psycho-physical discipline leading to concentration). *Jnana* focuses on knowing one's true being, which is one with the Absolute. One strays from one's true being because of ignorance. The knowledge that is sought after is not intellectual knowledge but experiential knowledge. This is attained through the study of the scriptures, reflection, and concentration that lead to experiential insight. *Bhakti* suggests that the unity with the Absolute is a relationship. The Absolute is personified. The relationship is one of love and self-surrender. Union is a gift of God. *Karma* envisages the universe as an ordered whole. One's duty is to play one's role in this universal process. This role was understood as ritual action at first. Later it was seen as moral action. Through appropriate action one integrates oneself with the universe or reality. *Yoga* is psycho-physical discipline that not only integrates the body and the spirit but also relates them in harmony with the energy field that is supra-corporal. It can be used as a preparation for the other ways. An experience of integration with reality through the body, mind, and energy can be seen as an end in itself. Some would say that these are not four different ways but four aspects of one way. In a particular tradition one or another aspect will be dominant. However, the goal that all these ways seek to lead toward is *advaitic* (non-dual) oneness with reality or being. The *advaita* should be seen not as one in a unitary sense, but as not-two or one-in-two or one-in-many. It is a unity in plurality. The egotism of humans, however, breaks up the unity and not only emphasizes the diversity but leads to fragmentation. Liberation, then, is seen as the effort to conform to or even to merge with reality that is one. Some Hindu traditions may suggest an "a-cosmic" approach of withdrawal from the world. The *sannyasis* quit the social order to pursue their goal of liberation *(moksha).* They are symbolically cremated at their initiation. They live in the world as if they are not in it. They pursue *moksha* single-mindedly, having abandoned the pursuit of other goals of life in the world, namely, *dharma* (righteousness), *artha* (wealth), and *kama* (pleasure). Others suggest the way of *nishkama karma* or desireless action in the world and in society. The popular *Bhagavad Gita* leads this tradition. One does what one has to do in conformity with the natural order of the universe or *dharma*. But one is not personally attached to that action or its consequences. One gives up egotism and attachment but not action. One surrenders oneself to the Absolute. Such desireless action seems close to the non-action of Taoism. The *dharma,* as the way in which the world functions, is very similar to the *tao.* Everything and every human in the universe has its *dharma*, which each has to follow freely and without attachment.

The Hindu tradition, however, unlike the Chinese one, lays more stress on reality or being than on the way. Though it speaks of four ways or *margas*, its goal is achieving oneness or union with the Absolute-Being. The end state is not *Tao* but Being. This leads one to be faithful to *dharma* or the way of Being. It envisages, for instance, *jivanmuktas,* people who have realized oneness with the Absolute in this life but who continue to live spontaneously conforming to *dharma*. The focus of *sadhana* or spiritual effort is not on the way but on the goal. The way is not given any importance in itself. Movement is seen as an imperfection. Being is beyond mobility and immobility.

Buddha's Eightfold Path

The Buddha summarizes his teaching in four noble truths. Life is full of suffering caused by the impermanence of everything. Suffering is caused by desire for or clinging to the impermanent things of the world. Liberation is to get rid of desire. To get rid of desire we have to follow the eightfold path. This consists of right understanding, right thought, right speech, right action, right livelihood, right effort, right mindfulness, and right concentration. The path leads one to liberation or *nirvana,* which means emptiness—that is, empty of anything perceived as permanent to which one may be tied through attachment. Looking at the eightfold path we can see it in three parts: *knowledge* of reality as impermanent, *life* that is unattached to the ever-changing reality, and *interiorization* of this freedom. Realization of the impermanence of reality involves giving up ego-centeredness and its attachments. One learns to accept events as they come. One is moved to compassion for those who are not yet free. The whole of life becomes the way to *nirvana*.

The Way of Israel

Though the story of Israel as described in the Bible starts with the story of creation, the covenant with Noah, and the journey of Abraham toward the land of promise, it seems to have a second start with the story of its experience in Egypt. The people of Israel are enslaved and oppressed. God calls Moses and sends him to liberate them (Ex 3). Under his leadership they run away from Egypt and march toward the promised land. They walk through the desert for forty years. They can be said to be on the way. During this time they also learn what it means to be the people of God. As they settle in the land of promise God gives them a vision of the community that God wants them to be. It is a community of equals who live together as God's children. Politically they are all under God, who is their only master. God foresees that they, in the course of ordinary life, will slip away from this ideal. Some will grow rich, and others will become poor. They may even be enslaved when they are not able to pay their debts. So God suggests a jubilee year, when social equality is re-established and they start again (Lv 25:8-55; Dt 15:1-18). During this year all debts are forgiven and all property is returned to the original owners. All slaves are freed. This can be seen as a symbol of universal reconciliation—though the law applies only to the Jews and not to the others who may be living among them.

But people are not happy with this way of life. They want to be like the other peoples around them. Their constant confrontation with those around them and perhaps their own efforts to expand made them tighten their organization. They organize themselves as a kingdom with a human king. They build God a temple and establish rituals and festivals. Their focus shifts from community life to politics and ritual observance. They overlook the fellowship and justice that should characterize community.

Through the prophets God recalls them to the basic principles and demands of community life. Through Hosea, God says:

> For I desire steadfast love and not sacrifice,
>   the knowledge of God rather than burnt offerings.
>   (Hos 6:6)

Referring to their habit of fasting as a sign of humility and penance, the Lord says through Isaiah:

> Is not this the fast that I choose:
>   to loose the bonds of injustice,
>   to undo the thongs of the yoke,
> to let the oppressed go free,
>   and to break every yoke?
> Is it not to share your bread with the hungry,
>   and bring the homeless poor into your house,
> when you see the naked, to cover them,
>   and not hide yourself from your own kin? (Is 58:6-7)

But the people do not really change. They even go after false gods. They are driven into exile, and they are subjugated to foreign rulers.

At the time of Jesus the people are under the foreign yoke of the Roman Empire. Their own leaders continue to exploit them. The priests and the elders gathered in the Sanhedrin use and promote the Temple and the rituals as a source of political authority under the Romans. They collect the Temple tax. They do not hesitate to use the Temple for financial gain by encouraging commercial activity within its precincts. The Pharisees present themselves as models of loyalty to God. But their focus is on the literal application of the laws of purity and pollution and of the Sabbath observance that forbade any kind of work on the day of rest. They are not interested in promoting fellowship and social justice.

The Way of Jesus

It is in this context that we must understand the way proposed by Jesus. He does not indulge in any metaphysical speculations. He does not speak much about nature as an element in his way, though he refers to nature as an example in many of his parables. The framework of Jesus is a human community fragmented by egotism and pride embodied in structures of religious, social, and political power. People are called to turn away from this self-centered arrogance. This is achieved through the selfless love of others, shown in humble service and sharing. This community is not something given but something to be created. God the Father, Jesus, and the Spirit are at the heart of this community-building. The community is therefore in God, divine. In God we reunite with the whole of the cosmos. The way of Jesus therefore operates at the level of human and social relationships. It is future oriented and dynamic. It is community centered. It resonates with the *nishkama karma* of the Indian tradition and the *wu wei* of the Chinese tradition. But it is set in a framework of cosmic-human-divine community building. The disciples, particularly John and Paul, will identify and elaborate this framework further. Let me now unpack and elaborate this brief description of the way of Jesus.

Jesus starts his public life with the proclamation: "The kingdom of God has come near; repent and believe in the good news" (Mk 1:15). George Soares-Prabhu points to the characteristics and dynamic movement of this kingdom:

> When the revelation of God's love (the Kingdom) meets its appropriate response in man's trusting acceptance of this love (repentance), there begins a mighty movement of personal and societal liberation which sweeps through human history. The movement brings *freedom* in as much as it liberates each individual from the inadequacies and obsessions that shackle him. It fosters *fellowship*, because it empowers free individuals to exercise their concern for each other in genuine community. And it leads on to *justice*, because it impels every true community to adopt the just societal structures which alone makes freedom and fellowship possible.[1]

Soares-Prabhu insists that Jesus does not propose a ready-made structure or blueprint. He is offering a vision and a way:

> The vision of Jesus indicates not the goal but the way. It does not present us with a static pre-fabricated model to be imitated, but invites us to continual refashioning of societal structures in an attempt to realize as completely as possible in our times the values of the Kingdom . . . Lying on the horizon of human history and yet part of it, offered to us as a gift yet confronting us as a challenge, Jesus' vision of a new society stands before us as an unfinished task, summoning us to permanent revolution.[2]

The kingdom of God that Jesus announced and began to establish is not an institutional, politico-military structure. It is a community of people who are ready to love and forgive, share, and serve. Each one of us is born in a family. We grow up and become what we are in relation to a group of people. We are mutually dependent. We are meant to live together and find happiness in being together. Obviously, such a community cannot be established once and for all. Every person who is born into the world has to become a member of it by his or her own free will. The process will go on as long as history continues. This kingdom is not otherworldly. It is a different way of being and relating to the others in this world. We are not waiting for it to happen after death. It is an actuality now. It is not merely spiritual and transcendent. It is human and historical, even earthly. It is an ongoing, dynamic process. It is not merely human. It embraces the whole universe to which humans are related through their bodies.

The Way of Love

The way to construct this community, according to Jesus, is love. It is a force that leads us outward to relate to the other. It is physical at the level of material elements and instinctive at the level of the animals. At the level of humans, given their consciousness and freedom, it becomes a personal relationship. It is gift that is given and received. It is free. It can be spontaneous. It is a human experience, at once physical, emotional, and intellectual. Through love a community of humans becomes a communion. A communion involves a sharing of all that one is and all that one has. It is a communion of life. Being human, it is free. It is not natural or automatic. It has to be built up, constructed.

The freedom to love and to build communion also implies the possibility of saying no. People can be self-centered. Their attempt to possess things may deprive others of what they need. Some may tend to treat others as objects and use them for their own satisfaction without respecting their individuality and freedom. They enslave and dominate them. Egoism and domination can be built into social structures like slavery and the caste system or today's free market. Women in general are socially oppressed. The society in which we live, therefore, is not the ideal community that we wish to have.

What should we do to move from a situation of inequality and injustice? We have to free people so that they can love. This freedom is not merely the spontaneity with which one acts. It also involves freedom from egoism and power. One has to become selfless and humble. Given the situation of inequality and injustice in which we live, people are bound to be hurt by the attitudes and actions of those who are selfish and dominant in society. Community building in such a situation supposes a capacity to forgive and be reconciled. Inequality and injustice are not only individual but also social and structural. So social movements and struggles for liberation may be necessary to bring about a transformation. Such struggles will have to be nonviolent if our aim is not to succumb to a spiral of violence, but both to liberate the oppressed and to challenge oppressors to conversion and change so that together all can construct a new community of equality and justice. In the meantime, some of those who struggle may have to suffer for the cause at the hands of the dominant group.

Loving God in the Other

A look at the life and teachings of Jesus shows us that his way of love includes all these elements.* It also sets them in a transcendent (or divine) context. Matthew narrates the following story:

> A lawyer asked him a question to test him. "Teacher, which commandment in the law is the greatest?" He said to him, "'You shall love the Lord your God with all your heart, and with all your soul, and with all your mind.' This is the greatest and first commandment. And a second is like it: 'You shall love your neighbor as yourself.'" (Mt 22:36-39)

In the story as narrated by Luke, the lawyer continues to ask who his neighbor is. Jesus replies to it with the parable of the Good Samaritan (Lk 10:30-37). The neighbor is someone who is alive to the need of another and goes out to help that person, undeterred by any consideration of economic, social or ritual status. Jesus, however, seems to merge the two commandments into a single one when he tells his disciples after the Last Supper: "This is my commandment, that you love one another as I have loved you" (Jn 15:12). He calls it a "new commandment" (Jn 13:34). The newness may be precisely in the fact that he drops the first commandment about loving God. The reason is that it is in the neighbor that we love God. He explains this in his story about the final judgment reported by Matthew. At the end of the world, when everyone will be gathered before him, the Son of Man

> will say to those at his right hand, "Come, you that are blessed by my Father, inherit the kingdom prepared for you from the foundation of the world; for I was hungry and you gave me food, I was thirsty and you gave me something to drink, I was a stranger and you welcomed me, I was naked and you gave me clothing, I was sick and you took care of me, I was in prison and you visited me." Then the righteous will answer him, "Lord, when was it that we saw you hungry and gave you food, or thirsty and gave you something to drink? And when was it that we saw you a stranger and welcomed you, or naked and gave you clothing? And when was it that we saw you sick or in prison and visited you?" And the king will answer them, "Truly I tell you, just as

---

* In the following paragraphs I am repeating material that I have already taken up in the previous chapter, though I am looking at it from a different point of view. This being a central element in the life and teaching of Jesus, such repetition cannot be avoided, especially as each image stands on its own.

you did it to one of the least of these who are members of my family, you did it to me." (Mt 25:34-40)

This story makes it clear that in helping the poor and the needy neighbor one helps and encounters the Lord. Love of God and love of others are not two separate activities. We love God *in* the others. John understood this well:

> God is love, and those who abide in love abide in God, and God abides in them . . . Those who say, "I love God," and hate their brothers or sisters, are liars; for those who do not love a brother or sister whom they have seen, cannot love God whom they have not seen. (1 Jn 4:16, 20)

Love in Service and Reconciliation

In his life Jesus shows what loving really means. His new commandment is framed between two significant events in his life. Before giving the commandment to love he gives an example of humble service by washing the feet of his disciples and by exhorting the disciples that they too should wash one another's feet (Jn 13:1-15). His words: "Learn from me, for I am gentle and humble in heart" (Mt 11:29) then become credible. After the commandment he comments on it by saying: "No one has greater love than this, to lay down one's life for one's friends" (Jn 15:13). Then he goes on to give an example of this by giving his own life. He symbolizes this by the sharing of food and drink at the Last Supper. Food is a symbol of life. To share food is to share life. In the symbols of bread and wine, Jesus shares his own body and blood. To eat together is also an expression of equality and community, further strengthened by the symbolic gesture of the washing of the feet.

In a human world, where there is an interplay of limited freedoms, mutual offense is inevitable. To love in such a situation is to be ready to forgive. Indeed, as we saw in Chapter 3, Jesus insists on the need to forgive.

A Nonviolent Struggle

In a situation of ritual and sociopolitical oppression in the Palestine of his time, where the poor, the sinners, the prostitutes, and the publicans are marginalized, he opts to be friendly with them (Mt 9:10-13) and challenges and condemns the rich (Lk 6:24-25). He criticizes the greedy priests by driving out the buyers and sellers in the Temple (Mk 11:15-18). He defies the Pharisees by healing people on the sabbath (Jn 5:2-18; Mt 12:1-14). The leaders of the Jews decide to get rid of him precisely because he is challenging their oppressive authority (Jn 11:45-53).

In struggling against the oppressive social and religious structures of his day, the way of Jesus is one of nonviolence. Protesting against oppression, he is ready to suffer for the cause of freedom and justice. He is against any violence, "for all who take the sword will perish by the sword" (Mt 26:52). Nonviolence respects the humanity and freedom of the oppressors and seeks to change them rather than treat them as objects by violently destroying them. The goal is not the victory of the oppressed over the oppressors, but the restoration of justice, equality, and fellowship for all, who will then live and work together as a community. The nonviolent reaction to oppression shocks the oppressors into rethinking their stand and challenges them to come to the negotiating table to discuss reform and reconstruction. Jesus, however, seems to be aware that such a transformation is not always possible immediately in history.

A Transcendent Way

The way of Jesus is not something apart from the way of the world. It is not something separate or different. But Jesus gives it a new meaning or significance. An example makes this clear. Sharing food and drink is a common symbol in many cultures. It signifies fellowship and equality. But when a Christian community shares food and drink in memory of Jesus and his paschal mystery of death and resurrection, Jesus becomes present in the food and drink, adding depth to the fellowship. It is a symbolic celebration. But it is not a new thing. Whenever people love one another, God is there sustaining and deepening their relationship. The divine is not the human. The divine is not something added on to the human either. It is a deepening or divinizing of the human. It is always there. In a sacrament like the Eucharist it is symbolically realized and celebrated. The way of the human is the way of the divine. We love God in the other means also that we love the other in God. God here is not an addition. We may ignore God. We may not be aware of God. But God is there always, even when not recognized. Therefore, the way of Jesus is at once human and divine. It does not alienate the human in order to make it divine.

Once the way is recognized as divine, then what disappears at death is only the historical conditionings in which the way has so far been appearing. It is now manifesting itself in a new manner. As long as we are walking on the way, we do not have to worry about this further dimension. It will take care of itself.

The fact that Jesus rises again from the dead adds a special dimension to the way of Jesus. We think of the resurrection as coming after death. But what Jesus seems to imply in some of his discourses is that there are dimensions in life that are not subject to death. This means that, on the one hand, the risen life starts now. On the other hand, the communion of love may not be achieved in this historical life. It starts here and now. But through a process of suffering and even death its fulfillment may be in the future that transcends history.

Jesus himself spells this out in *advaitic* terms. He says: "The Father and I are one" (Jn 10:30). Again, "Whoever has seen me has seen the Father . . . Believe me that I am in the Father and the Father is in me . . . The one who believes in me will also do the works that I do" (Jn 14:9, 11-12). Jesus prays to the Father "that they may all be one. As you, Father, are in me and I am in you, may they also be in us" (Jn 17:21).

An Inclusive Way

His disciples John and Paul point to other dimensions of this way of communion. Paul sees it as inclusive in two ways. In his letter to the Romans he suggests that the whole cosmos is involved and transformed in the process of community building:

> The creation waits with eager longing for the revealing of the children of God; for the creation was subjected to futility, not of its own will but by the will of the one who subjected it, in hope that the creation itself will be set free from its bondage to decay and will obtain the freedom of the glory of the children of God. We know that the whole creation has been groaning in labor pains until now; and not only the creation, but we ourselves, who have the first fruits of the Spirit, groan inwardly while we wait for adoption, the redemption of our bodies. (Rom 8:19-23)

The community of Jesus is not only human and divine but cosmic. In his letter to the Ephesians he sees the process of history as the plan of God "to gather up all things in him [Christ], things in heaven and things on earth" (Eph 1:10; see also 1 Cor 15:28). In his letter to the Colossians he calls it "the fullness": "For in him [Christ] all the fullness of God was pleased to dwell, and through him God was pleased to reconcile to himself all things, whether on earth or in heaven" (Col 1:19-20). The way of Jesus then is a cosmic process, in which not only humans but the whole universe are caught up. It is transhistorical, embracing and transcending the whole of history. It is the dynamic movement of history.

Paul's image for this cosmic unity is the body—the body of Christ (1 Cor 12:12-31). The force that unifies the body is love. Paul is sensitive to the very practical character of this love:

Love is patient; love is kind; love is not envious or boastful or arrogant or rude. It does not insist on its own way; it is not irritable or resentful; it does not rejoice in wrongdoing, but rejoices in the truth. It bears all things, believes all things, hopes all things, endures all things. Love never ends. (1 Cor 13:4-8)

John seeks to lay the groundwork that underlies such a cosmic communion by taking us back to creation.

In the beginning was the Word, and the Word was with God, and the Word was God. He was in the beginning with God. All things came into being through him, and without him not one thing came into being. What has come into being in him was life, and the life was the light of all people . . . The true light, which enlightens everyone, was coming into the world . . . And the Word became flesh and lived among us, and we have seen his glory, the glory as of a father's only son, full of grace and truth . . . From his fullness we have all received, grace upon grace. (Jn 1:1-4, 9, 14, 16)

Let me note in passing that John here links to Jesus the attributes truth and life, besides light, which Jesus also attributes to himself in conjunction with the way. Jesus tells the disciples: "I am the way, and the truth, and the life" (Jn 14:6). Jesus had claimed earlier to be the light of the world, linking it also to the way: "I am the light of the world. Whoever follows me will never walk in darkness but will have the light of life" (Jn 8:12). We need not go into the metaphysics of all this, except to point out how similar this is to the Chinese assertion that the way of humans is the way of Nature and the way of Heaven. The way of Jesus is the way of creation. It is the way of what is, what happens in reality. That is why it is the truth: what is. It is the way that humans and the world live. It is the life. It is God's gift to creation and to humanity. We can understand why some Chinese theologians call Jesus the *Tao*. But the *Tao* of Jesus has a Confucian resonance because it concerns community building.

The way of Jesus is the way of the cosmos starting with creation. It is the way of love. The life, death, and resurrection of Jesus clarify further and strengthen this way, which involves struggle and suffering that lead to reconciliation. Life is the enduring reality. It corresponds to the reality or truth of the cosmos. That is why when Jesus says that he is the way, the truth, and the life, these are not three different things. They are three aspects or three ways of looking at the same thing. The way points to the dynamic and process dimension of the truth (what is). Life is nothing but walking along the way. Because it is egoless, it is free of desire and aggressive action. It is animated by the Spirit of God (Rom 8:14-17).

The Way and the Ways

People in this world seek for *moksha*, liberation and fulfillment. They have devised many ways to that goal. In the context of Jesus, the way, I would like to reflect on two of them. They are the ascetical and mystical ways.

People are aware of their sinfulness (egotism and pride) and of their sinful deeds. They may have a consciousness of guilt. They find in penance a way out of this feeling of guilt. On the one hand, penance or self-imposed suffering, like fasting, can help control one's egotism and desire, following the principle of *agere contra* or acting against. Penance can also be thought of as doing reparation for one's sins. Penance can have a role as an element in the process of emptying oneself. Jesus fasted for forty days before he started his public ministry. But after that he does not seem to speak about it as a part of his way. John the Baptist had a reputation for an ascetic way of life. But Jesus does not follow the way of John. As a matter of fact, the disciples of John ask Jesus why his disciples do not fast as they and the Pharisees do (Mt 9:14-17). While praising John, he also contrasts himself with him. "For John came neither eating and drinking, and they say, 'He has a demon'; the Son of Man came eating and drinking, and they say, 'Look, a glutton and a drunkard, a friend of tax-collectors and sinners'" (Mt 11:18-19). Jesus does not ask his disciples to fast but to love and serve one another.

It is often said that the way of Jesus is the way of the cross. Jesus indeed suffered. But the suffering was imposed on him. He did not go after it. He was ready to suffer for the sake of love and justice—in defense of his principles. But I do not think that he saw self-imposed suffering as a special way to the goal of life as he had outlined it, namely, the kingdom of God as a community of freedom, fellowship, and justice. Penance can have a preparatory role. But it should not be exaggerated.

There is a lot of interest in methods of meditation. People speak of a mystical way as opposed to the ascetical way. Hindu methods like yoga and Buddhist methods like Zen are very much in demand. As a matter of fact, most of the techniques are based on yoga. There are various levels. Regular and slow breathing and exercise of metal concentration that empties the mind of its roving thoughts and fantasies can bring a feeling of relaxation and mental and emotional peace. This appeals to many people in a world where people are suffering from various kinds of stress in the family, in the market, and in the work place. Sometimes people try to go beyond this and get in touch with the energy field that animates and surrounds our bodies and also links it to other sources of energy. While a lack of balance in this energy field leads to many psychosomatic illnesses, a balancing of the energy field can lead to healing. At a further level people may have an experience of going beyond their normal consciousness when their center of awareness shifts from the body-mind to the energy field. People may even have out-of-body experiences. Finally, people may feel that in transcending the body and the energy field they have touched the Absolute spirit or Being. Some experts consider yoga a natural human experience. Others feel that it is a step to the experience of the Absolute. While some may believe that this experience of the Absolute is natural and automatic, others, who believe in a personal Absolute, think that, while we can prepare ourselves through concentration, the Absolute can be experienced only by those to whom the Absolute chooses to manifest itself.

These various meditation experiences may sound very complicated. People can aim at any one of the levels that I have indicated. Theological and spiritual background and motivation and effort may make people interpret their experiences in various ways. While a Buddhist experiences emptiness and a Hindu experiences non-duality, a Christian experiences the fullness of God. I am not saying that the same experience is interpreted differently. They may be different experiences, depending on attitude, motivation, and faith context. It is not my purpose here to elaborate on these.

If we believe that God is in us and we are in God, it is natural that some want to experience this in a human way. Since the relationship is real, I think that an experience of it is possible. But since the relationship is the encounter of two freedoms, God's and the human's, I think that the experience cannot be automatic. It can be prepared for elaborately, waiting on God, so to speak. God can also choose to give it suddenly without any preparation, overwhelming the person in the process. The experience is possible—we have the writings of mystics that testify to such experiences—and aspiring to such an experience is legitimate.

What I suggest here is that mystical ways that go beyond relaxation techniques are for the few who feel called to them and who have the time and energy to undertake the effort. But for people in general, including mystics, the real way to fulfillment is the way of Jesus, the way of selfless love and service. It is the way accessible to everyone in the world as it is, here and now. It is the natural way of life in community that extends to include the cosmos. Ignatius of Loyola has a phrase that I have always found attractive: finding God in all things and all things in God. We experience God in the world and in the other. Loving God in the other, we love the other in God. This involves mystical insight and contemplation. We do not need elaborate

5

Jesus,
the Guru

The term *guru* is a common one in Indian languages. It has become common today even in other languages. It is used popularly to refer to a teacher. More properly, it refers to a guide. Used in a spiritual context, it refers to those who have walked along the way and have experienced, or at least have had a glimpse of, the goal one is looking for. Therefore they are capable of guiding disciples *(sishyas)* in their own search. They can initiate them and lead them along the path that they have trod themselves. They can instruct them, solve their doubts and difficulties. They can authenticate their experiences. It is traditional in India that gurus do not go out looking for disciples. On the contrary, it is the disciples who seek a guru, someone competent to guide them along their spiritual path because of the guru's prior experience of having walked successfully along that path.

Normally, gurus instruct and train their disciples and, when they are ready, initiate them. When disciples are formally initiated, they pursue their own path. Some may in turn become gurus. This is how a tradition is built up. Of course not every disciple becomes a guru. One must qualify through personal experience and recognition by others. When the disciples are not full-time searchers, but only seek out the guru for occasional advice, the guru-*sishya* relationship becomes a continuing one. In some modern *ashrams*, patterned on European monasteries, the guru-*sishya* relationship is institutionalized and permanent.

In the *advaitic* (non-dual) tradition, in which true spiritual experience consists in realizing one's oneness with the Brahman or the Absolute, gurus are seen as divine, because they have experienced *advaitic* oneness with the Divine. They are called Bhagavan or God, like Bhagavan Ramakrishna or Bhagavan Ramana Maharishi. In the Bhakti traditions like Saiva Siddhanta, in which the final experience is one of encountering Siva, the Absolute, in love, Siva himself is seen as reaching out to the devotee or disciple as a guru or through a human guru. It is not clear whether the guru in such an encounter is a special manifestation of Siva or is Siva acting through a human mediator. In any case the guru can be a divine-human person.

My purpose here is not to explore the various shades of meaning of the term *guru* in the Indian tradition, but rather to see whether, taken in a general sense, it can help us to understand aspects of Jesus. Many Indian disciples of Jesus, whether Hindu or Christian, have considered him as their guru. Christians stress the uniqueness of Jesus by calling him *sadguru* (true guru). It is a comparative term. But I am not adopting a comparative approach in this book. I am only exploring various images that can lead us to a deeper understanding of Jesus in relation to us. I think that guru is one such image. From this point of view gurus are guides who can initiate and lead disciples to fulfillment because they themselves have experienced it.

When we look at Jesus as guru, one easy approach could be to see him as divine and quote a text like: "The one who comes from heaven is above all. He testifies to what he has seen and heard" (Jn 3:31–32). As a divine person, Jesus knows what he is talking about. So he is a real guru. But this is not the way that the disciples and others actually experienced him. They experienced him as primarily human. As human, he "increased in wisdom and in years, and in divine and human favor" (Lk 2:52). He was not born a guru. He became one and acted as one. But he was not universally accepted. When Jesus spoke of his own body as the living bread from heaven, "many of his disciples turned back and no longer went about with him" (Jn 6:66). Others accused him of being an agent of the prince of demons (Mk 3:22). Still others refused to accept his authority because he came from Galilee and did not observe strictly ritual prescriptions like the sabbath observance (Jn 9:16). We can see his development as a guru in the gospels.

The Formation of a Guru

Jesus must have grown up in Nazareth frequenting the synagogue on the sabbath day, as any good Jewish boy would do. As a young adult he hears about John the Baptist and goes to meet him in the desert. I do not suppose that he just walked into the water one fine morning to be baptized by John. He must have listened to his teachings. During this encounter his personality must have struck John in some way, because he hesitates to baptize him (Mt 3:14). But he did not see too clearly, since he needed to send his disciples later to Jesus to ask him: "Are you the one who is to come?" (Lk 7:19). Jesus, however, must have had a sense of special vocation at the moment of his baptism by John so that he heard a voice that said "You are my Son, the Beloved; with you I am well pleased" (Lk 3:22). Both this special sense of vocation and the example of John the Baptist drove Jesus into the desert for a period of penance and trial. He fasted, prayed, and was tempted.

The gospels tell us about three kinds of temptations. First of all, since he is hungry, he is asked to command a stone to become bread. He is tempted to use any powers he may have been given in view of his mission to satisfy his own needs and desires. Jesus answers: "One does not live by bread alone, but by every word that comes from the mouth of God" (Mt 4:4). Then he is asked to throw himself down from the pinnacle of the Temple, trusting that God will save him through the angels. This is a temptation to egotism, projecting his own self-importance and forcing God to acknowledge it. It betrays also a sense of insecurity. Jesus answers: "Do not put the Lord your God to the test" (Mt 4:7). Finally he is promised the whole world if he worships Satan. He is promised power over everything. His rebuke is sharp: "Away with you, Satan!" (Mt 4:10). These temptations are probably not three particular events, but rather three types of tests. Luke, for instance, adds: "When the devil had finished every test, he departed from him until an opportune time" (Lk 4:13). So the trials must have continued.

Matthew reports one such trial. Jesus asks his disciples what people think about him. They say that he is commonly perceived as a prophet in the line of Elijah, Jeremiah, and John the Baptist. Then Jesus asks: "But who do you say that I am?" Peter answers for everyone: "You are the Messiah, the Son of the living God" (Mt 16:13–16). After this confession, Jesus tells them about the sufferings that he will have to face in Jerusalem. Peter takes the liberty of rebuking him: "God forbid it, Lord! This must never happen to you." The sharp reaction from Jesus is similar to the one in the desert: "Get behind me, Satan!" (Mt 16:21–23). We have other similar stories. Jesus visits his hometown, Nazareth. He goes to the synagogue and reads the famous text from Isaiah

> "The Spirit of the Lord is upon me,
>   because he has anointed me
>   to bring good news to the poor"

and declares, "Today this scripture has been fulfilled in your hearing." The people expect him to do some miracles there as he did in Capernaum. He refuses to oblige them and they try, unsuccessfully, to throw him off a cliff (Lk 4:16–30). At another time the Pharisees ask him for a sign from heaven. He tells them, "No sign will be given to this generation" (Mk 8:12). As Jesus hangs on the cross, everyone around tempts him. The Jewish leaders scoff at him: "He saved others; let him save himself if he is the Messiah of God!" (Lk 23:35). The soldiers mock him: "If you are the King of the Jews, save yourself!" (Lk 23:37). One of the criminals crucified with him derides him: "Are you not the Messiah? Save yourself and us!" (Lk 23:39).

A New Model

The people at the time of Jesus have an ideal vision of what a Jewish guru should be. The rabbis, who comment on the scriptures and the law, and the Pharisees, who claim to observe all the prescriptions of the law faithfully, are their models. Jesus refuses to conform to those models. He proposes a new vision of the law that insists on interiority and authenticity. He insists on purity of intention and attitude rather than mere external conformity. He suggests praying and fasting in secret rather than making a show of it so as to be praised by others (Mt 6:1–6). He breaks cultic practices, like the literal observance of the sabbath, and shows that the needs of the people have priority (Mt 12:1–14). He transgresses their social and ritual restrictions and their purity-pollution taboos when he eats and drinks with the sinners and the tax collectors (Mt 9:10–13). He suggests faithfulness to the spirit of the law rather than to its letter. Though he visits the Temple regularly, as all Jews do, and even pays his Temple tax (Mt 17:24–27), he protests vigorously against the Temple's abuse for commercial purposes by driving out buyers and sellers (Mk 11:15–17). His life and teaching do not go unchallenged. The Pharisees suggest that he drives out demons by the help of their ruler, Beelzebub (Mt 9:34). The leaders question his authority to teach and to heal (Mt 21:23). On the one hand, these encounters clarify to Jesus and to the others open to listening to him that the way to God is not through faithful observance of ritual and law but through fidelity to the fundamental demands of a love that reaches out preferentially to the poor and the oppressed. The encounters strengthen Jesus. On the other hand, they set him on a collision course with the Jewish authorities, who see his actions as a challenge. The crowds that follow Jesus make the Jewish leaders suspect that their authority over the people may be slipping. And so they are keen to take action against him (Jn 11:47–53). Jesus is also aware of the coming confrontation. He knows the destiny of the prophets. He has seen the violent end of John the Baptist. And yet, when the showdown comes near, he is afraid. He prays: "Abba, Father, for you all things are possible; remove this cup from me; yet, not what I want, but what you want" (Mk 14:36). Acceptance and love conquer fear, and he surrenders himself. But he is only too aware that "the spirit is indeed willing, but the flesh is weak" (Mk 14:38). He cries out while hanging on the cross: "My God, my God, why have you forsaken me?" (Mk 15:34). Still, he forgives his persecutors praying, "Father, forgive them; for they do not know what they are doing" (Lk 23:34). He also reassures the "good" thief: "Today you will be with me in Paradise" (Lk 23:43). Finally, his surrender is total and unconditional: "Father, into your hands I commend my spirit" (Lk 23:46).

As we have seen in Chapter 2, many Asians (Indians) who look on Jesus as a guru focus on his moral teachings, such as those compiled by Matthew in his Sermon on the Mount (Mt 5—7). Only Mahatma Gandhi takes his passion and death on the cross seriously as an example of nonviolent struggle.

A Pilgrim Guru

I have said above that a guru has had the experience of the Absolute and therefore can initiate and guide others on their way. The picture we have of Jesus is slightly different. He certainly experiences the call of God and the power of God with him in view of his mission. He must have felt his communion with his Father strongly in his moments of prayer. We read in Mark's gospel: "In the morning, while it was still very dark, he got up and went out to a deserted place, and there he prayed" (Mk 1:35). Luke tells us: "Now during those days he went out to the mountain to pray; and he spent the night in prayer to God. And when day came, he called his disciples and chose twelve of them, whom he also named apostles" (Lk 6:12–13). Prayer, therefore, precedes important decisions. His transfiguration—during which his chosen disciples, Peter, James, and John, see him in the company of Elijah and Moses and hear a voice saying: "This is my Son, the Beloved; listen to him" (Mk 9:7)—must have been a peak experience, strengthening him for his coming suffering. However, such an experience of communion with the Father is not a fulfillment experience achieved once and for all. It coexists with an ongoing struggle that is particularly sharp during the passion and the death on the cross.

His experience and his competence to guide others develop and are perfected in the course of his life through his various encounters. Such encounters happen, not only with enemies who keep challenging him, but also with others who surprise him with their faith and draw out his resources. At the marriage feast at Cana, Mary simply informs him, "They have no wine" and then tells the servants: "Do whatever he tells you," in spite of his seeming protest (Jn 2:3–5). A centurion surprises him by his faith, suggesting that he can cure his servant just by a word of command (Mt 8:5–13). A woman with a flow of blood seems to get a miracle out of him by touching his cloak without out his knowledge (Lk 8:43–48). The Canaanite woman counters his arguments with her assertion that even the dogs eat the crumbs that fall from the master's table (Mk 7:24–30). And Zacchaeus's curiosity to see him is a sign of his readiness for conversion (Lk 19:1–10).

This process, however, does not prevent him from choosing and forming his disciples. But his teaching for them will be completed only when they encounter the risen Jesus. Jesus becomes the complete guru only with the resurrection. The disciples too acquire a fuller grasp of the teachings of Jesus when they look back at them in the light of the resurrection.

Guru and Disciples

In Indian tradition a guru who goes about hunting for disciples is looked on with suspicion. It is the disciples who seek out a guru, attracted by the guru's example and way of life. In the case of Jesus we see a variety of ways in which the disciples come to the guru. John tells us of two of John the Baptist's disciples who hear John's witness and follow Jesus. Jesus tells them, "Come and see." They go, see, and stay with him. One of them, Andrew, brings along his brother Simon, and Jesus names him Peter or "the Rock" (Jn 1:35–42). The following day Jesus calls Philip, who in his turn brings Nathanael. Nathanael, skeptical at first, is impressed by Jesus and stays with him (Jn 1:43–51). Matthew speaks of Jesus calling Andrew and Peter, and then James and John, while they were fishing (Mt 4:18–22). Luke makes the incident more dramatic. The four had been fishing for a whole night without success. Then Jesus gives them a tip and they haul in a lot of fish. Peter has enough experience of fishing to realize that this was no ordinary tip and exclaims, "Go away from me, Lord, for I am a sinful man." Jesus then reassures him and the others that "from now on you will be catching people" (Lk 5:8–10). Jesus calls Matthew while he is sitting at the tax booth (Mt 9:9) but confirms his desire to reach out to sinners and tax collectors by participating in a feast at his house (Mt 9:10–13). On the part of Jesus there is a call. On the part of the disciples there is a possibility of experience before a final decision to join him.

Jesus has a number of women followers too. Luke gives us the list: "Mary, called the Magdalene, from whom seven demons had gone out, and Joanna, the wife of Herod's steward Chuza, and Susanna, and many others, who provided for them out of their resources" (Lk 8:2–3). Obviously these women were much better off financially than the poor fishermen. Many others wish to follow Jesus but are deterred by other pressing concerns. One does not like the wandering life of Jesus. Another has to go and bury his dead father (Mt 8:21–22). Jesus insists on a single-minded orientation. "No one who puts a hand to the plow and looks back is fit for the kingdom of God" (Lk 9:62). Still another has too much wealth, which he does not want to give away (Mt 19:16–22). Mark even says, "Jesus, looking at him, loved him" (Mk 10:21). That love does not overcome the person's freedom and force him to follow Jesus.

Among his many disciples Jesus specially chooses twelve. Mark says, "He appointed twelve, whom he also named apostles, to be with him, and to be sent out to proclaim the message, and to have authority to cast out demons" (Mk 3:14–15). Matthew adds, "and to cure every disease and every sickness" (Mt 10:1). This corresponds to what Jesus himself was doing. What is the significance of this group?

Guru of an Apostolic Social Movement

Jesus experiences the opposition of the Jewish leaders. He feels that it is gaining strength and that he himself may not be around too long. But he wants his work of proclaiming the arrival of the kingdom of God and of calling people to conversion to continue. The number twelve refers probably to the twelve tribes of Israel, thus making this a representative group and a new people of God. The apostles are chosen to give a new push to the old mission of God, aimed at sharing God's life with people and integrating them as a community. Jesus trains these twelve in a special way. When Judas abandons the group, becoming the betrayer of Jesus, the group replaces him with Matthias, thus emphasizing the symbolic nature of the number twelve. The condition that they lay down is interesting. He should be "one of the men who have accompanied us during all the time that the Lord Jesus went in and out among us, beginning from the baptism of John until the day when he was taken up from us" (Acts 1:21–22). This means that there were many others, besides the apostles, who were faithful disciples of Jesus. As a matter of fact, Jesus sends seventy others "to every town and place where he himself intended to go" (Lk 10:1). However, the twelve do seem to have a special role among these disciples.

The ultimate realization or final fulfillment that Jesus was moving toward was not merely a personal one that can be repeated in the case of other persons under his guidance. He seems to have in mind a social project—a new community, a new people of God. He seems to be aware that this social project will continue after his death and resurrection. He foresees a fulfillment to come in the near or distant future. Paul and John will see this fulfillment as universal reconciliation or communion (Eph 1:3–10; 1 Cor 15:28; Jn 17). The foreseen goal is double. Every person reaches personal fulfillment. But this is part of the fulfillment of all. We can recall here the Buddhist bodhisattva ideal in which the bodhisattva—a person who has attained liberation or fulfillment—postpones its completion in order to help others attain final liberation so that at the end everyone is fulfilled together. As a guru, Jesus is not merely guiding people toward personal fulfillment. He is launching and animating a global project that works for the fulfillment of all humans and of the whole universe. The project of Jesus is therefore both personal and social/cosmic. It embraces the whole of history till God is all in all (1 Cor 15:28). Jesus is therefore the guru of a cosmic movement that he initiates himself and perpetuates by choosing disciples and sending them to continue his mission. His training of his disciples, therefore, is not only to seek personal fulfillment but to work for the fulfillment of all. This is his ideal of the kingdom of God.

The Vision of the Kingdom

Jesus spells out his vision of the kingdom particularly in the parables. He often starts his parables with a phrase: "The kingdom of heaven is like . . . " The parables do not offer us a systematic teaching about the kingdom. They present different strokes of the brush, highlighting different aspects. Let me try to put them together. The best image of the kingdom in the gospels is that of the wedding banquet (Mt 22:1–14). It focuses on a family and a wide circle of friends. It is a community celebration embodied in a common festive meal, expressive of joy and fellowship. The king, being the host, invites everyone to participate. Starting with the more important people, the invitation finally reaches every one. What dominates the image of the banquet is community.

Bringing such a community together is not a political project. It is not achieved by an army. It is enabling people with freedom to come together and to relate to one another in spite of the many economic, social, political, and cultural factors that divide them. Jesus sees that this work of conversion and reorientation leading to relationship will have to be done quietly from within. That is why he compares the emergence of the kingdom to the growing of a seed (Mt 13:1–9, 31–32). The image of the seed has the advantage of pointing to the interaction between the seed and the soil in which it grows. We shall come to this point later. A seed has the possibility of growth. A small mustard seed can become a big tree (Mt 13:31–32). Jesus also compares the kingdom to leaven. "The kingdom of heaven is like yeast that a woman took and mixed in with three measures of flour until all of it was leavened" (Mt 13:33). The dynamic power of the kingdom transforms from within, almost unseen.

A seed cannot grow without the soil. God has created humans as free beings. God does not impose community on us. We have to build up the community freely. God sows the seed, but it grows in us who are the soil. Our responses may vary from nil to one hundred percent. The basis of this response is the giving up of our egotism and pride and reaching out to the others in community. If we really understand and appreciate the vision of community that God is proposing for us, then we will be ready to abandon everything in order to pursue the vision actively. Jesus underlines the need for such readiness to give up everything by evoking two images:

"The kingdom of heaven is like treasure hidden in a field, which someone found and hid; then in his joy he goes and sells all that he has and buys that field. Again, the kingdom of heaven is like a merchant in search of fine pearls; on finding one pearl of great value, he went and sold all that he had and bought it." (Mt 13:44–46)

In the story about the poor widow who donates two copper coins to the Temple treasury, Jesus points out that all one has need not be much in worldly terms (Mk 12:41–44). What matters is the intention to give everything one has. In another parable Jesus talks about the king who gives five, two, and one talent, respectively, to three of his servants according to their ability. The king expects them to use their talent(s) productively; this is important, not the quantity of the product (Mt 25:14–30).

While God expects us to do what we can, God's gift is conditioned only by God's own generosity. We have the parable about the master who sends servants into his vineyard at all hours of the day till the last hour and then pays everyone equally at the end of the day. His recompense is not measured by the work put in but by his own generosity, on the one hand, and perhaps also by the needs of the workers and their dependents, whatever amount of work they were able to do (Mt 20:1–16). What can block God's forgiving love and generosity is our own self-sufficiency. People who think that they are materially or religiously rich—Pharisees, in their own estimation—do not need God. The rich man did not take note of the poor Lazarus till he found him in the bosom of Abraham (Lk 16:19–31). In the parable of the Pharisee and the tax collector who go to the Temple to pray, we see the contrast. The Pharisee compliments himself for his good behavior, whereas the tax collector confesses his sin. It is the tax collector who goes home justified (Lk 18:9–14). There are other self-sufficient people in the parables, such as the rich man who has a good harvest and is looking forward to enjoying it without realizing that he will die that very night (Lk 12:16–21). Jesus opts for the sinners and the tax collectors, not because they are good, but because they are aware of their sinfulness and open to conversion. The sinful woman who washes the feet of Jesus with her tears and wipes them with her hair at the house of the Pharisee and Zacchaeus, who shares his goods, are examples of this (Lk 7:36–50; 19:1–10).

Jesus makes it clear that the community he envisions among humans and with God is rooted in love. In the parable of the Good Samaritan (Lk 10:25–37), he points out that love is shown in sharing and service of others, especially those who are in need. Given the situation of selfishness and fragmentation in the world, Jesus shows that the first step in the process of loving is forgiving. Jesus presents God as a forgiving parent. The parables of the prodigal son, of the shepherd who goes in search of the one lost sheep among a hundred, and of the woman who searches for the lost coin (Lk 15) show that God is ready to forgive us and reintegrate us into the community. The forgiving God encourages us also to forgive one another, loving even our enemies (Mt 5:43–48). The link between the two is expressed in the prayer that Jesus teaches his disciples: "And forgive us our debts, as we also have forgiven our debtors" (Mt 6:12). He elaborates this in another parable. A master forgives a servant who is unable to pay his debt. But then the servant goes out and refuses to forgive another servant who owes him money. The master is furious and punishes the first servant (Mt 18:23–35).

Community building will not be a smooth project because it will be resisted by people who are selfish and proud. So history will be a process of ongoing tension. The parable about the weeds and the wheat points this out (Mt 13:24–29). But history will also be a process of continuing challenge. Opportunities for building community will present themselves at any moment, and we will always have to be ready. The parables present this in an eschatological language: the king who comes back to demand an account. The king will arrive unexpectedly. So we always have to be ready. The parables about the ten bridesmaids and about the faithful and unfaithful slaves illustrate this (Mt 25:1–30). This eschatology must not be understood as something in the distant future. The language of the future is symbolic of a continuing and dynamic present. So we have to be accountable at each moment. God is forgiving for those who repent. But he is not irresponsible. He will take us to task. The parables about the barren fig tree (Lk 13:6–9) and the wicked tenants show this (Mt 21:33–41). The vineyard is God's. We are sent there as trustees. We are accountable to what we do with it. We have no claim to ownership. It is interesting that this idea of stewardship is spoken of today in the context of ecology. The Lord has entrusted the earth to humanity. It is meant for all, not to be exploited unjustly by a few. This idea of accountability brings us back to the parable of the banquet with which we started this account of the parables (Mt 22:1–14).

The king invites the rich people for a feast. But they are caught up in their own selfish interests: land, animals, marriage. Then the king throws open the gates to everyone. But this does not mean that people can come to the banquet without the appropriate attire. It means to be ready because the call may come at any time.

All of us are invited to build the kingdom together with God and with others. We cannot really opt out of it. It is what gives meaning to our lives. But we should not have grandiose dreams. Clarity about our capacity and our possibilities is also necessary. Prudence and discernment are indicated (Lk 14:28–32). At the same time, building community in a world that is unjust will lead us into conflict and suffering. It is in this context that we have to understand the warning of Jesus:

> "Do not think that I have come to bring peace to the earth; I have not come to bring peace, but a sword . . . Whoever loves father or mother more than me is not worthy of me; and whoever loves son or daughter more than me is not worthy of me; and whoever does not take up the cross and follow me is not worthy of me. Those who find their life will lose it, and those who lose their life for my sake will find it." (Mt 10:34, 37–39)

The Demands of Discipleship

Being the disciple of Jesus does have some basic demands. One has to be with him, living with him, learning from his teachings and actions and even being trained by him in a special way. One leaves everything to follow Jesus. Jesus himself asks the rich young man who asks his advice: "Go, sell your possession, and give the money to the poor . . . then come and follow me" (Mt 19:21). The disciples had done that. Peter says: "Look, we have left everything and followed you" (Mt 19:27). Jesus confirms this when he says: "Everyone who has left houses or brothers or sisters or father or mother or children or fields, for my name's sake, will receive a hundredfold" (Mt 19:29). Discipleship also demands personal commitment. After a long discourse about eating his flesh and drinking his blood so as to have a share in his divine life, Jesus sees many of his disciples leaving him, saying, "This teaching is difficult" (Jn 6:60). So Jesus turns to the twelve and asks, "Do you also wish to go away?" Peter, as usual, answers for all: "Lord, to whom shall we go? You have the words of eternal life. We have come to believe and know that you are Holy One of God" (Jn 6:67–69). Thomas gives dramatic expression to this commitment. The proposal of Jesus to go back to Judea after the death of his friend Lazarus encounters resistance at first, because the Jews in Judea had sought to stone Jesus. But when Jesus insists, Thomas says to his fellow disciples bravely, "Let us also go, that we may die with him" (Jn 11:16). As a matter of fact, when the showdown actually arrives, all of them will run away. Peter will deny knowing him three times, and John will follow him "at a safe distance." But that they gather again in the upper room waiting for something to happen shows that they have a certain basic loyalty to the group and to the project for which Jesus has trained them.

Speaking of the disciples of Jesus we should not overstress the twelve, whatever their symbolic and institutional role in the community. It can never be an exclusive one. Peter's talk to the group after the ascension to choose a replacement for Judas shows that other disciples besides the twelve followed Jesus.

Such other disciples included women, some of whom were economically and socially better off. They may have been at the Last Supper. They were the first to go to the tomb on the third day after the death of Jesus and encounter him. Mary Magdalene stands out among these. There were hidden disciples like Nicodemus and Joseph of Arimathea. There were householders like Martha, Mary, and Lazarus. They were sympathetic outsiders like the centurion, the Canaanite woman, and the Samaritan woman. When we think of the Last Supper and the appearances after the resurrection of Jesus, we tend to focus only on the twelve. Maybe we are influenced by institutional concerns and/or pictures of the Last Supper like those of Leonardo da Vinci. The Acts of the Apostles tell us that the apostles "were constantly devoting themselves to prayer, together with certain women, including Mary the mother of Jesus, as well as his brothers" (Acts 1:14). I am sure that when the Holy Spirit came on Pentecost, it came on all of them gathered there. Jesus probably met the same group in the upper room after the resurrection when he breathed the Spirit on them and sent them on a ministry of reconciliation. The women were probably funding the whole operation, as they had done during the lifetime of Jesus. Working back from these facts we could project that the disciples, male and female, were at the Last Supper too. They must have come to Jerusalem accompanying Jesus. The Passover meal was a family meal, to which everyone was invited. The women would have looked after the provisions and arrangements—and the service, except for the washing of the feet by Jesus. On the other hand, even among the twelve, he seems to have given special roles to Peter, James, and John. Peter was their spokesman. These three are chosen to witness the transfiguration (Mk 9:2–8) and the agony in the garden (Mk 14:32–42). They must have been sensitive to this privilege. Peter presumes to protest when Jesus speaks of his impending passion (Mt 16:22) and when he is washing his feet (Jn 13:6). When Jesus speaks of their abandoning him, Peter is the loudest in denial: "Even though all become deserters, I will not . . . Even though I must die with you I will not deny you" (Mk 14:29, 31). James and John, on the other hand, request special places by the side of Jesus in the coming kingdom (Mk 10:37). Jesus will teach them both by word and example that special roles do not mean special honor but rather special responsibility and special suffering.

Training in Mission

Even during his lifetime Jesus sends his disciples on mission to announce the coming of the kingdom of God. He sends, not only the twelve (Mt 10:5), but also another seventy later (Lk 10:1). He empowers them, not only to proclaim the good news of the arrival of the kingdom, but also to do the symbolic works that he did of healing and exorcism. He stresses the gratuity of their ministries. They are expected to stay with the people wherever and whenever they are welcome, enjoying their hospitality, but never forcing their presence on anyone. They have to preach in poverty: "Take no gold, or silver, or copper in your belts, no bag for your journey, or two tunics, or sandals, or a staff" (Mt 10:9–10). They are not to impose the good news on unwilling listeners either. They must be ready for opposition and persecution, depending on the Spirit of God to inspire them at that moment on how to behave themselves and what to say, because they are doing God's work. The disciples go out and have a very successful mission (Lk 9:6). They were astonished at their own success. Jesus warns them not to be proud of their success, because they have been doing the work of God. He takes the occasion to give them a lesson in humility by praying to the Father: "I thank you, Father, Lord of heaven and earth, because you have hidden these things from the wise and the intelligent and have revealed them to infants; yes, Father, for such was your gracious will" (Lk 10:21).

Jesus also teaches them by example. The biggest lesson is, of course, his own passion and death. He does not flinch at the sufferings imposed on him by the leaders of the Jews and, at their behest, by the Romans. He witnesses to his mission and to his convictions unto death. He did exhibit his fear and vulnerability at the beginning. But once the process starts, he takes in his stride betrayals and false witnesses and refuses to compromise. It was also an example of total abandonment of himself into the hands of God, trusting that God will justify him. Though the disciples run away while he is facing his trial, they learn the lesson rather quickly. Acts tells us that "they rejoiced that they were considered worthy to suffer dishonor for the sake of the name" (Acts 5:41).

There were many other minor examples during his public life. His miracles of healing and exorcism would have been, in general, a lesson in being sensitive to the suffering of others. When a big crowd comes to him in the desert and the apostles suggest that he send the people away to look for food, he makes them collaborate with him in feeding them miraculously. In their presence he defies the Pharisees and scribes regarding their narrow, literal, and uncaring interpretation of the law. When they dispute among themselves about who is the greatest, Jesus, "aware of their inner thoughts, took a little child and put it by his side, and said to them, 'Whoever welcomes this child in my name welcomes me, and whoever welcomes me welcomes the one who sent me; for the least among all of you is the greatest'" (Lk 9:47–48). At another time, when the disciples seek to "protect" him from the "nuisance" of little children, he says: "Let the little children come to me, and do

not stop them; for it is to such as these that the kingdom of God belongs"
(Lk 18:16). He also sternly warns those who cause scandal to little children,
suggesting that they should be thrown into the sea with a millstone around
their neck (Lk 17:2). He rebukes James and John, who suggest command-
ing fire to come down and consume a Samaritan village that refuses them
hospitality. His free mixing with Samaritans and others considered sinners
by the Jews was an example, both of considering each person equal as a
child of God and of a preferential love for the poor, the oppressed, and the
marginalized. His table fellowship with such people may have been one of
the inspirational sources for the Eucharist later.

He teaches them the importance of faith and prayer when he heals a
spirit-possessed boy whom the disciples could not heal (Mk 9:14–29). He
seems to test and form their faith when he calms the storm (Mt 8:23–27)
or walks on the water, inviting Peter to do the same (Mt 14:22–33). His own
frequent prayer at night or early morning must have been an example to
them, though the only time that he invited three of them—Peter, James, and
John—to join him in prayer in the garden, when he needed their special
support, they fell asleep (Mk 14:32–42). They do, however, ask him to teach
them to pray, and Jesus teaches them the Our Father (Lk 11:1–4). Made up
of praise and petition, it has become a model prayer. It can also be seen as
a summary of the mission on which Jesus is sending them. God's name will
be holy and God's will will be done on earth as in heaven when the kingdom that Jesus and the apostles proclaim becomes a reality. The kingdom
is God's own mission and God's own doing. God is gracious to seek our
collaboration as free humans. But, finally, it is God's grace that will achieve
it. The kingdom is the human community that God is building on this earth.
God provides the earthly sustenance necessary for the community. God promotes universal reconciliation by setting us a model of forgiveness. In an
ongoing conflict between the forces of good and evil, God empowers us to
withstand evil. These petitions remind us that it is all God's doing, though
even God cannot achieve it without our collaboration. The key to this understanding is that God's forgiveness becomes real in our forgiving one another. Just as we love God in others, in reconciling with others we are reconciled with God. Forgiving others we too are forgiven. Our agency is
respected, though God is the ultimate agent. The model prayer that Jesus
teaches the disciples becomes a summary vision of the cosmic kingdom.

A Careful Teacher

Jesus is not an esoteric teacher. He does not have one kind of teaching
for the crowd and more secret instructions for the disciples. Matthew makes
this clear: "When Jesus saw the crowds, he went up the mountain; and after

he sat down, his disciples came to him. Then he began to speak, and taught them" (Mt 5:1–2). He is teaching both his disciples and the people. But this openness does not exclude the possibility that the disciples, committed to him as they are and being with him all the time and listening to his various discourses, understand what he is teaching better than the others. Most people come to him for his miracles of healing. They have their own priorities. The thousands who were fed seek to make him king (Jn 6:1–15). When Jesus tries to explain the significance of sharing food as sharing life at a higher level, however, many abandon him (Jn 6:25–60). Others in the audience are people who are unsympathetic to Jesus, like the Pharisees and the leaders of the people, who feel their own vision and social domination threatened. Their eyes are closed, their hearing impaired, and their hearts hardened. They see but do not perceive; they hear but do not understand; they feel challenged but do not change (Mt 13:13).

Sometimes Jesus teaches in parables. We have seen these earlier. But he does not teach only in parables. His teachings collected by Matthew, for example, are quite clear and authoritative. In teaching in parables Jesus probably uses a strategy. He wants his hearers to make a little effort to interpret the stories. His disciples ask for an explanation, but others do not. So he explains the parables to his disciples. It is not that the Pharisees did not know how to interpret stories. They spent most of their time trying to interpret the law in their own way. The problem was their perspective. Jesus warns his disciples to be careful not to adopt that perspective. He compares it to yeast. It can be good, of course, but it can be bad also (Mk 8:15).

It is a sad fact that in recent times a guru cult seems to be developing. The guru, rather than being a guide, seems to become the goal. The guru is divinized, and absolute obedience is demanded from the disciples. The disciples remain perpetual disciples. Even after death the guru's *samadhi* or tomb becomes an object of cult, and the now invisible guru becomes the center of the group. Authorized interpreters may bring in an element of hierarchy in the group. This was never the tradition of India/Asia. Even in Saiva Siddhanta, in which Siva himself was experienced as coming in the form of a guru, the historical manifestation will never be absolutized and divinized. This seems to have happened to some Indian gurus in recent times. It is unfortunate that similar temptations seem to be affecting some Christian *ashrams* too. Of course, it is not a new tendency. In Christian tradition the tendency has been to divinize the institution, the aura of which devolves on its current leaders.

A Case Study

In the story of the encounter of Jesus with the Samaritan woman (Jn 4:1–42) we have an example of how a guru should handle disciples, respecting their freedom and guiding them along to make basic choices in life. The method used is dialogue. The request for a drink by Jesus serves as the entry point for his conversation with the Samaritan woman. This simple request brings up the issue of the prevalent socioreligious discrimination in which the Samaritans are treated as religious and therefore also social untouchables. The water is used as a symbol to evoke the theme of life. The Samaritan woman is interested. But the reception of the water of life supposes some conditions or dispositions on her part. So she is gently led to face her existential situation, especially with reference to love and personal relationships. She is bold to accept her problematic situation of having had five husbands and now living with a sixth man. But she raises a more basic issue of religious discrimination based on different mediations and traditions of cult. Jesus relativizes the mediations and affirms the possibility of worshiping God anywhere in spirit and truth:

> The hour is coming, and is now here, when the true worshipers will worship the Father in spirit and truth, for the Father seeks such as these to worship him. God is spirit, and those who worship him must worship in spirit and truth. (Jn 4:23–24)

Nothing now hinders the Samaritan woman from making her surrender to the Messiah who is manifesting himself but at the same time leading her to worship of God in spirit and truth. The Samaritan woman, in her turn, becomes a guru, leading the villagers to encounter Jesus as the Messiah. But once the encounter takes place the mediation of the Samaritan woman is no longer relevant. In this story Jesus gives us an example of how a guru should operate. He himself is seen as a prophet who leads to the worship of God in spirit and truth.

A Special Guru

In India, when we speak of a guru, we have many images. One of them is a *sannyasi*. A *sannyasi* is someone who has renounced the world and left the social order to pursue single-mindedly the final goal of human life, namely *moksha* or liberation. He or she has no permanent abode but is a wanderer. When such gurus have some success in attaining their goal, disciples will seek them out to be trained and initiated and sent on to pursue their own individual paths. In modern times a guru is often associated with an *ashram*. The guru has a community of disciples. The guru is the center of the community. The disciples remain permanent disciples. Today the community of disciples may extend across the globe, and the guru may become a globe-trotting one.

Each guru teaches a particular way of achieving fulfillment in life—a *sadhana*. This may even be rigidly imposed on the disciples.

Jesus combines both these images but avoids their pitfalls. He is a *sannyasi*—a world-renouncer and a wanderer. He is also a guru with a community of disciples. But he has no *ashram*. He lives on the streets, the beaches, the mountains, and the deserts. He preaches by word, example, and action. To these two images, however, Jesus adds a third one. He also launches a social movement for personal and social transformation. His goal is not only to free people and make them integrated humans, but also to build community. Full personal integration is found precisely in relationship with the universe, with humans and with God. He gathers a group of disciples, male and female, to continue his work and to take the movement to the ends of the earth. His movement does not take people away from the world but is centered on life and community, although he insists on a certain detachment, so that one is in the world but not "worldly," loving without attachment and acting without desire.

Looking at Christian history, Francis of Assisi, Ignatius of Loyola, John Bosco, and a host of others could be considered such gurus. In Asia, Confucius and the Buddha are models. A more recent model is Mahatma Gandhi. Gandhi himself would consider Jesus his guru. He lived as a renouncer, had an *ashram* to train his group of disciples, and launched a national movement of personal, social, and political liberation. It is the greatness of the guru Jesus that he can inspire other gurus.

6

Jesus,
the *Satyagrahi*

Satyagraha is a term coined by Mahatma Gandhi. *Satya* means truth. The root of the word *satya* is *sat*, which means "being." *Satya*, therefore, is what is. *Satya* as truth adds a moral connotation to being. "What is" is "what ought to be." Gandhi said that Truth is God. God is "who is." Considering God as truth has an advantage. Truth is an ideal that can be followed. We are expected to be true, to speak the truth, to do the truth. Even if it is difficult, we have to try. *Graha* means "clinging." *Satyagraha*, therefore, means "clinging to truth." Clinging expresses a stronger, more forceful action than following. It supposes commitment and determination. It can demand courage and persistence. A *satyagrahi* is someone who does *satyagraha*, who clings to truth, namely, to God.

Gandhi saw his own life as a quest for truth. He knew that truth is absolute. One does not possess truth; rather, one is possessed by it. So he saw himself as approaching truth in stages. Truth is not self-evident either. People's egotism and desire have spread falsehood on the earth. Truth, therefore, has to be discovered in life and in the world. It has to be discerned and identified at each moment. Its concrete manifestations can only be partial, limited by historical circumstances and the inadequacy of humans. Achieving truth through its partial manifestations in life and in history is a process. It is also a project. That is why Gandhi named his autobiography *My Experiments with Truth*—an experiment that never ends till death.

I said that truth is not merely "what is," but "what ought to be." Gandhi believed that a free, egalitarian, and just community of humans is "what ought to be." *Satyagraha* is therefore possible and necessary not only at a personal level but also at the social level. Gandhi, as a *satyagrahi*, sought to achieve truth and justice, not only in his personal life, but also in society. In the India of his time this meant not only freeing India from the colonial yoke of the British but also caring for the poor and promoting economic justice, liberating the dalits or "untouchables" and promoting social equality and justice, advocating love and avoiding violence of every kind, encouraging interreligious fellowship and harmony. Gandhi also firmly held that the ends do not justify the means. We cannot reach truth through untrue means. So freedom and justice in society can be promoted only through honesty and justice in personal life and in the means that one adopted. We cannot promote peace through violence.

My aim here is not to explain Gandhi's spiritual and political ideology and his sociopolitical movement. It is to understand the meanings that the image *satyagrahi* normally evokes in the Indian mind today. It is true that this image is linked to Gandhi's life and work. But today it is an image that is more widely understood. It has become a common noun, which can be applied to anyone who is searching for Truth. A *satyagrahi* is someone who is committed to freedom, truth, and justice and who engages in nonviolent sociopolitical action in order to achieve those values, both in personal and social life. When we look at Jesus and search for images to understand and give expression to his significance, *satyagrahi* seems one of them. My aim here is not to compare Jesus and Gandhi. Rather, it is to explore how Jesus struggled for freedom, truth, and justice in his own life. In his personal life he was constantly tempted to set his own self before the truth or God (Lk 4:1–13). In his public life he had to struggle against the sociopolitical and spiritual leaders of the Jewish people, namely, the priests, sadducees, and Pharisees. Gandhi may have coined the term *satyagrahi* in the twentieth century. But he did not discover the ideal. It was lived by Jesus nearly two thousand years earlier. Gandhi would be the first to recognize this. He considered himself a disciple of Jesus and a faithful follower of his teachings in the Sermon on the Mount, though he also rediscovered this ideal in the *Bhagavad Gita,* as interpreted by him.

The choice of the image *satyagrahi* points to the idea that Jesus, though he was a revolutionary, was a nonviolent one. Other images like liberator or revolutionary have been used to understand Jesus. The Latin American theology of liberation calls Jesus the liberator. Using tools of Marxist analysis of society, its focus, at least in the beginning, was economic and political. Spirituality was added later. There have also been efforts to include cultural analysis in recent years. In the Ecumenical Association of Third World Theologians culture came into the picture with the Africans and religions with the Asians. Our focus on liberation is integral, not merely economic and political, but also social and cultural, religious and personal. The image liberator points to the evil and injustice from which the poor and the oppressed people have to be set free. Though the kingdom of God is proposed as the ideal to follow, revolutionary violence is either tolerated or even encouraged as a response to the structural violence of the oppressors. The end is used to justify the means. Jesus himself is made a political revolutionary. The image *satyagrahi* is used to highlight a different way of looking at Jesus as a revolutionary.

A Prophet

Jesus was in the prophetic tradition. The Jews of his time looked upon John the Baptist as a prophet. John came to preach repentance. He did not mince his words: "You brood of vipers! Who warned you to flee from the wrath to come? Bear fruit worthy of repentance. Do not presume to say to yourselves, 'We have Abraham as our ancestor'; for I tell you, God is able from these stones to raise up children to Abraham" (Mt 3:7–9). Many people flocked to him to listen to his message and sought the baptism of repentance at his hands. Jesus himself went to be baptized by John. John, however, presented himself as a forerunner and foretold of another who was to come: "I baptize you with water for repentance, but one who is more powerful than I is coming after me . . . He will baptize you with the Holy Spirit and fire" (Mt 3:11). He seemed to have had some idea that Jesus was this person. When Jesus comes to him for baptism he says: "I need to be baptized by you, and do you come to me?" (Mt 3:14). According to John (the apostle), John the Baptist testifies: "I saw the Spirit descending from heaven like a dove, and it remained on him. I myself did not know him, but the one who sent me to baptize with water said to me, 'He on whom you see the Spirit descend and remain is the one who baptizes with the Holy Spirit'" (Jn 1:32–33).

The message of Jesus continued the prophetic tradition. It was also a call to conversion. As Mark reports to us briefly: "After John was arrested, Jesus came to Galilee, proclaiming the good news of God, and saying, 'The time is fulfilled and the kingdom of God has come near; repent and believe in the good news'" (Mk 1:14–15). The people recognize him as a prophet. When Jesus asks his disciples what people think about him they reply: "Some say John the Baptist, but others Elijah, and still others Jeremiah or one of the prophets" (Mt 16:14). Even Herod is said to be perplexed (Lk 9:7–9).

Jesus, however, was a special kind of prophet. We see two kinds of prophets in the Old Testament of the Bible. The earlier (pre-exilic) prophets called the people to conversion, but their point of reference was their liberation from Egypt and their covenant with God as God's people. Hosea is representative of others like Joel and Amos:

> When Israel was a child, I loved him,
> and out of Egypt I called my son.
> The more I called them,
> the more they went from me;

> they kept sacrificing to the Baals,
> > and offering incense to idols . . .
>
> They shall return to the land of Egypt . . .
> > because they have refused to return to me.
> The sword rages in their cities,
> > it consumes their oracle-priests,
> > and devours because of their schemes . . .
>
> How can I give you up, Ephraim?
> > How can I hand you over, O Israel? . . .
> My heart recoils within me;
> > my compassion grows warm and tender.
> I will not execute my fierce anger;
> > I will not again destroy Ephraim;
> for I am God and no mortal,
> > the Holy One in your midst,
> > and I will not come in wrath.
> > > (Hos 11:1–2, 5–6, 8–9)

God is disappointed at Israel's infidelity and yet is ready to forgive. But Israel persists in its idolatry and ends up in exile. We hear its longing for God and plea for forgiveness in the psalms:

> By the rivers of Babylon—
> > there we sat down and there we wept
> > when we remembered Zion. (Ps 137:1)
>
> As a deer longs for flowing streams,
> > so my soul longs for you, O God. (Ps 42:1)
>
> Have mercy on me, O God,
> > according to your steadfast love. (Ps 51:1)

The later (post-exilic) prophets condemn the continuing disloyalty of the people. Some of them may have been in exile with the people. They do not look back so much to the liberation from Egypt but rather look forward to a new kingdom of God to come. They spell out this newness in various ways. Isaiah promises:

> I will appoint Peace as your overseer
> > and Righteousness as your taskmaster.

Violence shall no more be heard in your land,
   devastation or destruction within your borders;
you shall call your walls Salvation,
   and your gates Praise.

The sun shall no longer be
   your light by day,
nor for brightness shall the moon
   give light to you by night;
but the LORD will be your everlasting light,
   and your God will be your glory. (Is 60:17–19)

The spirit of the Lord GOD is upon me,
   because the LORD has anointed me;
he has sent me to bring good news to the oppressed,
   to bind up the broken-hearted,
to proclaim liberty to the captives,
   and release to the prisoners. (Is 61:1)

For I am about to create new heavens
   and a new earth;
the former things shall not be remembered
   or come to mind . . .
The wolf and the lamb shall feed together,
   the lion shall eat straw like the ox. (Is 65:17, 25)

Jeremiah promises a new covenant: "I will put my law within them, and I will write it on their hearts; and I will be their God, and they shall be my people (Jer 31:33). Ezekiel evokes a valley of dry bones that are made alive by the Spirit of the Lord and goes on to promise: "I will put my spirit within you, and you shall live, and I will place you on your own soil" (Ez 37:14).

Jesus, like John the Baptist, comes in this tradition. But unlike John the Baptist, he is not speaking of a kingdom to come. He says, "The time is fulfilled and the kingdom of God has come near" (Mk 1:15). The announcement is more dramatic in Luke. Jesus goes to Nazareth, where he grew up. He goes to the synagogue and reads from Isaiah:

"The Spirit of the Lord is upon me,
   because he has anointed me to bring good news to the
      poor.

He has sent me to proclaim release to the captives
and recovery of sight to the blind,
to let the oppressed go free,
to proclaim the year of the Lord's favor." (Lk 4:16–19)

He then goes on to say:

"Today this scripture has been fulfilled in your hearing."
(Lk 4:16–21)

A Different Prophet

In the course of his life Jesus does indeed show that the kingdom of God has come near. The blind see, the lame walk, the hungry are fed. While proclaiming the blessedness of the poor, he condemns the rich:

Then he looked up at his disciples and said:
"Blessed are you who are poor,
for yours is the kingdom of God.
Blessed are you who are hungry now,
for you will be filled.
Blessed are you who weep now,
for you will laugh.
"Blessed are you when people hate you, and when they exclude you, revile you, and defame you on account of the Son of Man. Rejoice in that day and leap for joy, for surely your reward is great in heaven; for that is what their ancestors did to the prophets.
But woe to you who are rich,
for you have received your consolation.
Woe to you who are full now,
for you will be hungry.
Woe to you who are laughing now,
for you will mourn and weep."
(Lk 6:20–25; see also Mt 5:3–12; 23:13–36)

Jesus opts for the poor and the oppressed and condemns their oppressors, namely, the Pharisees and the leaders of the people (Mk 2:16). He transgresses their dietary laws and those concerning purity and pollution (Mt 15:10–20). He challenges their strict regulations regarding the sabbath observance and heals people on the sabbath (Mt 12:9–13). He defends the right of his disciples to eat the corn from the field on the sabbath (Mt 12:1–8). He drives the vendors from the Temple courtyards (Mt 21:12–13).

Jesus is also different from the prophets in another way. The prophets normally spoke in the name of God. Their messages normally started with "Thus says Yahweh." But Jesus teaches in his own name. "You have heard that it was said to those of ancient times . . . But I say to you . . . " (Mt 5:21–22). He teaches with authority. He does not oppose traditional teaching but deepens and interiorizes it. He goes beyond behavior to intention and motivation.

We are not told in the Bible that any of the prophets had a body of disciples who would continue his mission. But Jesus has a large body of disciples, both men and women. Some of the women seem to have been socially prominent ones, like the wife of Herod's steward (Lk 8:3). He organizes them in some way. He chooses twelve of them and sends them on a mission to proclaim the kingdom (Lk 9:1–6). At another time he sends seventy of them on a mission (Lk 10:1–12). The Jewish leaders must have seen this as a campaign or a movement. It was religious, but with political overtones. Religion and politics were not neatly distinguished in the Jewish tradition. This was not an armed gang of revolutionaries but poor people, including fishermen and a former tax collector, proclaiming blessings on the poor and woes on the rich and the powerful.

Besides his many other miracles of healing and forgiveness, his raising of dead people to life on three occasions—the daughter of Jairus (Lk 8:40–56), the son of the widow at Naim (Lk 7:11–17), and Lazarus, his friend (Jn 11:1–44)—and his calming of the storm in the sea (Mk 4:35–41; 6:47–52) are symbolic of the peace and the life that the kingdom brings. They also indicate his power over nature.

His invitation to the kingdom and his call to conversion are not heeded. Even the people of his own village reject him (Mt 13:54–58). Some ask for a sign (Mt 16:1). They are not satisfied with his miracles of healing. They probably expect some cosmic manifestation with thunder and lightning as happened when Israel was in the desert (Ex 19:16–20). The leaders question his authority, which does not flow from their institutional structures. By referring to John the Baptist he indicates that his authority is prophetic, from God, not institutional (Mt 21:23–27). They test him with questions like the one about paying taxes to the emperor. He asks them to show him a coin that has the emperor's image on it and coolly declares, "Give to the emperor the things that are the emperor's" (Mk 12:17). He also foresaw that he would be treated like other prophets, that is, rejected and killed (see Mt 23:29–36; 16:21–23). He actually warns his disciples of coming persecutions: "As for yourselves, beware; for they will hand you over to councils; and you will be beaten in synagogues; and you will stand before governors and kings because of me, as a testimony to them" (Mk 13:9).

The leaders of the people are perturbed and plot against him. John reports to us:

> So the chief priests and the Pharisees called a meeting of the council, and said, "What are we to do? This man is performing many signs. If we let him go on like this, everyone will believe in him, and the Romans will come and destroy both our holy place and our nation." But one of them, Caiaphas, who was high priest that year, said to them, "You know nothing at all! You do not understand that it is better for you to have one man die for the people than to have the whole nation destroyed." (Jn 11:47–50)

It is not unusual for leaders to think that their interests are the people's interests. It is not unusual either for one person to be sacrificed for the presumed good of everyone. It is also clear that this is a political decision.

Once the decision is taken, then strategies are planned. They find Judas to help them arrest Jesus without a crowd of people around him. They do not find credible witnesses. So they confront him with their direct question, "Are you the Messiah?" When he answers in the affirmative, instead of discussing it they accuse of him of blasphemy. This accusation also helps them get the Romans involved by accusing Jesus of pretending to be the king of the Jews. Jesus does not seek to avoid confrontation with the authorities. It is true that he is not the kind of Messiah for whom they were waiting. But they have no time to talk about it. He has taken the role of a prophet, and he is ready to face the consequences. It is not that he is happy to suffer. He would have been happy if the cup of suffering had been removed from him. But he trusts in God and stands firm, ready to face the suffering.

The End of the Conflict

The scenario unfolds as the Jewish leaders had planned. Pilate seems to hesitate for a moment. But political wisdom wins over any concern about truth. Truth becomes a casualty in the process. In the light of our choice of *satyagrahi* as an image for Jesus, it is interesting to look at the conversation between Pilate and Jesus, with its reference to truth:

> Then Pilate entered the headquarters again, summoned Jesus and asked him, "Are you the King of the Jews?" Jesus answered, "Do you

ask this on your own, or did others tell you about me?" Pilate replied, "I am not a Jew, am I? Your own nation and the chief priests have handed you over to me. What have you done?" Jesus answered. "My kingdom is not from this world. If my kingdom were from this world, my followers would be fighting to keep me from being handed over to the Jews. But as it is, my kingdom is not from here." Pilate asked him, "So you are king?" Jesus answered, "You say that I am a king. For this I was born, and for this I came into the world, to testify to the truth. Everyone who belongs to the truth listens to my voice." Pilate asked him, "What is truth?" (Jn 18:33–38)

Pilate does not wait for an answer. He has no patience to hear about truth. He is not keen on pursuing it. But he is sharp enough to realize that the accusation against Jesus is false, whatever the truth of his being king in another realm. "He went out to the Jews again and told them, "I find no case against him" (Jn 18:38).

Then Jesus is mocked, flogged, and crucified. The cause of the crucifixion is displayed on the cross: "Jesus of Nazareth, the King of the Jews." The efforts of the Jewish leaders to correct this—"He *claimed* to be the King of the Jews"—does not cut any ice with Pilate. Jesus remains true to character when he prays, "Father, forgive them; for they do not know what they are doing" (Lk 23:34). They were not interested in pursuing truth; they were busy with their game for power.

The story has a happy ending from the point of view of Jesus—when he rises again, appears to various disciples, and sends them on their mission to proclaim and build up the kingdom of God (Mk 16:9–20). The story does not end but continues. The life story of Jesus on the earth may have ended, but the story of the kingdom of God continues. Now the agents or the bearers of this story are the poor and the oppressed that Jesus empowered by his sufferings, death, and resurrection. So the story continues as an unending—ongoing—revolution. The quest for truth continues. The song sung by Mary on another occasion can now be sung by everyone:

> "His mercy is for those who fear him
>> from generation to generation.
> He has shown strength with his arm;
>> he has scattered the proud in the thoughts of their
>>> hearts.
> He has brought down the powerful from their thrones,
>> and lifted up the lowly;
> he has filled the hungry with good things,
>> and sent the rich away empty." (Lk 1:50–53)

A Nonviolent Conflict

Movements for a violent revolution were not unknown at the time of Jesus. There were the Zealots. What distinguished Jesus from the Zealots were two things. The Zealot effort focused on liberating Palestine from the colonialism of the Romans. They wanted a free Palestine. On the contrary, Jesus does not seem to focus much on the Roman presence in Palestine. He takes it for granted. When the Pharisees try to trap him by asking him, "Is it lawful to pay taxes to the emperor?" Jesus asks to see the coin that is in common use. They show him a Roman coin. Then he answers: "Give therefore to the emperor the things that are the emperor's, and to God the things that are God's" (Mt 22:21). Jesus points out, not too subtly, that, as long as they are using the Roman coins, they are acknowledging their subjection to the Roman emperor.

The focus of Jesus is much more on the Jewish community and the internal oppression that the poor suffer at the hands of the political (the chief priests and the leaders) and religious (the Pharisees) elite. These mediate the Roman oppression. He is worried about the day-to-day injustice suffered by the people. He is bothered by the divisions and hatred that afflict them. He is concerned about building a basic human community of freedom, fellowship, and justice, one that can exist irrespective of the prevailing political order. So he speaks about justice, forgiveness, and love in human relationships. He is not advocating any particular political order. A loving and sharing human community can be lived within any political system. Waiting for an ideal political system cannot be an excuse for not living in community. Perhaps a community will be born precisely in opposing an unjust political system and struggling for freedom and equality. It is not that just any political system is acceptable to Jesus. But an unjust political system need not be an alibi for refusing to live in community. All political systems have their drawbacks. Any political system can be manipulated by people with money and power—as the contemporary "democracies" bear witness.

The second difference between him and the Zealots is the means used to promote revolution. Jesus is firmly committed to the means of love and nonviolence. He wants socio-structural transformation. But he wishes to bring it about through personal transformation of attitudes and relationships. He knows that even a nonviolent revolution cannot avoid some violence from the oppressors. But he refuses to inflict it on anyone, though he is ready to undergo it in pursuit of the values he stands for and in their defense.

Nonviolence, for Jesus, is both a means and a strategy. He believes that the end does not justify the means. The ends and means must be homogenous. We cannot promote love through hatred, nor peace through violence.

Only love can provoke love in the other. Violence provoked by violence can lead only to a spiral of violence not to peace. But violence, undergone patiently and lovingly for a cause, can be creative. It provokes others to think and eventually to change. Thus violence undergone becomes a nonviolent strategy.

People who favor violent revolution often bring forward the example of tyrants who are madly violent. They mention people like Hitler or Stalin. Such tyrants may not feel challenged by the suffering of the people whom they are persecuting. They are focused only on their goals and consider people expendable. But even they might feel challenged if others with a conscience, bystanders or people whom they claim to be protecting—for example, non-Jews in Germany under Hitler or "good" communists in the Soviet Union under Stalin—protest and are ready to accept suffering in solidarity with the victims. No dictator rules alone. There are always a lot of camp followers, who benefit in their own way from the situation. They are collaborators. Then there is the silent majority. Its members do not want, not only to say no evil, but also to see no evil and to hear no evil. At the least they are ego-centered and unconcerned about others. At worst, they are afraid for themselves, their families, their property, their convenience. It is the silence of such non-victims that leave the victims defenseless before tyrants.

The Meaning of Suffering

It is almost taken for granted in many cultures and religions that suffering is punishment for evil. The theory of *karma* in Asian religious traditions supposes this. Most penal systems accept the principle. It was common in the Old Testament. We see this in the book of Job. Everyone, including Job, takes it as a matter of course that suffering is punishment for sin. Only God refuses to accept this principle. As we have seen earlier, the apostles bring forward this principle to understand the blindness of the man born blind and ask Jesus whose sin it is due to, his own or his parents. Jesus refuses the principle and suggests that the blindness will be an occasion to reveal the glory of God (Jn 9:2–3). When the disciples were faced with the suffering and the death on the cross of Jesus, they look for an explanation. They wish to affirm the salvific value of the suffering of Jesus. The paradigm that comes to their mind is the ritual of the scapegoat. The sins of the people are placed on its head and it is driven into the desert. They also have the example of sacrifices of atonement (Lv 16). The Jews see their own sufferings as punishment for their sins. Fear of God's anger and expiating one's sins and guilt with a sacrifice of an animal are common in the cosmic religions. So they find the meaning for the suffering of Jesus within this paradigm. Of course Jesus is sinless. So he is suffering for the sins of humanity.

Jesus, as we saw, refused this paradigm. His paradigm is one of love and self-gift. One shows love by giving oneself. Accepting death for another can be a symbol of total self-gift. Soldiers offer their lives to save others and to defend the honor of their country. Parents may offer their life to save their child. Readiness to offer one's life for the other shows the depth of one's love and commitment. As Jesus said, "No one has greater love than this, to lay down one's life for one's friends" (Jn 15:13). Love was the central paradigm of his life and teaching. It is in this context that we must interpret the gift of his life represented by his suffering and death.

God, the Father of Jesus, is not a vengeful God who demands expiation for sins. Jesus presented God as a loving and forgiving parent. The suffering imposed on Jesus comes not from God but from the Jewish leaders who seek to defend their own self-interest by doing away with Jesus. Jesus does not want to suffer. Jesus is against the violence done to the victims. He does not condone it or consider is praiseworthy. He is protesting against violence, whether physical, mental, or spiritual, done to the poor, the oppressed, and the marginalized of his day. But if his opposition to such violence brings violence and suffering on himself, he is ready to undergo them precisely as a sign of protest. His readiness to die shows the depth of his love and commitment to God and to the people.

His self-gift acquires special value when God responds to his love by the gift of life in raising him from the dead, by sharing with him God's own life. It is this response of God that makes his death significant for salvation. God's response saves. Just as the self-giving cross of Jesus challenges each one of us—egotistic sinners in our own way—to conversion and self-gift, his resurrection is a promise of new life to each one of us. This is a continuing process, so that the cross-and-resurrection event becomes a paradigm in history and in the lives of people.

In a nonviolent struggle, suffering accepted out of love for the oppressor also has a strategic value. The sufferer's hope is that the oppressors, however hardhearted they are, insofar as they are human, will be challenged to rethink their attitudes and presuppositions and thus be led to change.

From Conflict to Negotiation

In the concrete this might lead to negotiation and discussion. We see this happening soon after the death of Jesus. Acts tells the story. The murder of Jesus by the Jewish leaders does not put an end to the movement that he has launched. As a matter of fact, it acquires new vigor. The new community feels empowered by its experience of the risen Jesus. Though the disciples had run away when Jesus was arrested, now they are ready for any suffering. So they continue the work of Jesus without fear. They are brought before the Jewish council. They argue their case. The council lets them go with a warning (Acts 4:1–22). The apostles do not stop their work. They are picked up again. The Jewish leaders want to kill them (Acts 5:33). But one among them, Gamaliel, intervenes and counsels prudence. He tells them: "Keep away from these men and let them alone; because if this plan or this undertaking is of human origin, it will fail; but if it is of God, you will not be able to overthrow them—in that case you may even be found fighting against God" (Acts 5:38–39). He is listened to, and the apostles are set free after a flogging and a warning. The Romans do not enter the picture at all at this stage. The whole matter seems less political. But the Romans will intervene in the case of Paul, when he appeals to them. In the meantime the community has grown strong, and the Jews are already fighting a losing battle.

Where was Gamaliel when Jesus was condemned? For that matter, where were Nicodemus and Joseph of Arimathea? Maybe they spoke up in the assembly of the Jewish leaders but were brushed aside. Maybe it was a hurried or manipulated meeting and they were not there.

Love, Forgiveness, and Nonviolence

Gandhi often said that nonviolence looked at positively is love. The teaching and action of Jesus illustrate this. Jesus had made "love one another" his new commandment. He presented it as the sum and summit of all the commandments. He had shown that true love is expressed in humble service (washing the feet of his disciples) and sharing food and life (the Last Supper). He had also said that "no one has greater love than this, to lay down one's life for one's friends" (Jn 15:13). But his teaching went even further. In the Sermon on the Mount he said:

> You have heard that it was said, "An eye for an eye and a tooth for a tooth." But I say to you, Do not resist an evildoer. But if anyone strikes you on the right cheek, turn the other also . . . Love your enemies and pray for those who persecute you, so that you may be children of your Father in heaven; for he makes his sun rise on the evil and on the good, and sends rain on the righteous and on the unrighteous . . . Be perfect, therefore, as your heavenly Father is perfect. (Mt 5:38–39, 44–45, 48)

What the Sermon on the Mount does not point out is that loving the enemy is not merely an attitude of perfection but also a force for transformation, both for oneself and for the enemy. It is more usual to hate one's enemy. In loving the enemy one rises above the principle of retribution and becomes like one's Father in heaven. The enemy too, seeing an unexpected reaction, is challenged to rethink his or her attitudes and approaches. The enemy may let go of prejudice and ignorance regarding the other. This lays the groundwork for a new relationship.

To love is also to forgive. In his miracles of healing, Jesus manifests the Father's forgiveness. He tells the paralytic: "Take heart, son; your sins are forgiven . . . Stand up, take your bed and go to your home" (Mt 9:2, 6). The Jews focus on the authority that Jesus claims to forgive sins, since God alone can forgive sins. In the process they do not see the link between sickness and sin. Sickness is not punishment from God for sin. But it can often be the psycho-physiological manifestation of the tensions generated by one's own sinful attitudes and behavior like anger, hatred, depression, and egotism. Forgiveness removes the cause of sickness and heals. In this way forgiveness causes personal transformation.

Jesus places the practice of forgiveness at the center of the lives of the disciples. He teaches them to pray:

"Forgive us our debts,
as we also have forgiven our debtors." (Mt 6:12)

It is the equivalent of "love one another as I have loved you" (Jn 15:12). Forgiveness, like love, is limitless (Mt 18:21–22). Then there is the example of Jesus on the cross: "Father, forgive them; for they do not know what they are doing" (Lk 23:34). Forgiveness does away with one's own hurt and resentment. It also frees the others from feelings of guilt. Thus it promotes reconciliation and peace, transforming both sides and creating a new relationship in the process. The way of nonviolence is a way of love and forgiveness.

Nonviolence is a way of life. It is not merely an effective strategy in sociopolitical conflicts. It is a way in which we relate to others in families, in the community, and among friends and coworkers. Wherever people relate to or interact with one another, the way of nonviolence is not only relevant but necessary to promote peace and harmony.

The Cross as a Sign of Victory

The cross of Jesus acquires a special meaning when he is seen as a *satyagrahi*. The cross is often said to be a scandal to the Greeks. The Asians do not accept a suffering divine person. This is quite understandable if suffering is seen in a negative way as punishment for sin. People normally want to avoid such suffering. It is not something to be proud of. It is deserved. But if suffering is a sign of self-gift, then it is something to be proud of. Then there is no reason why a divine person should not suffer.

Suffering and death are imposed on Jesus by the Jewish leaders. More than as punishment they see them as preventive measures that save them and the people from reprisals by the Romans. They think that it is better that one man suffers so that the many may be spared. At least this is how they justify their imposition of suffering on Jesus. He is not suffering on their behalf. He is suffering so that they may be safe. But Jesus accepts the suffering as the consequence of his prophetic challenge to the leaders of the Jews. The suffering adds weight to his prophecy. It is a manifestation of his commitment to truth and justice. He is ready to suffer and die for his principles. His suffering adds force to his challenges. For him, suffering is not a sign of weakness or surrender. It is a sign of courage and strength. A person who suffers and dies for a cause should not attract our pity or commiseration but provoke our admiration. The suffering becomes transformative. It transforms the person who suffers. He or she is not a victim but a martyr. The suffering is no longer meaningless. It makes rather a very public and challenging statement. It represents the greatest force that the person who suffers can give to it. The person thus becomes the living and dying symbol of the cause for which he or she is suffering. It is the high point of the struggle. The person is the hero. Others not only admire such a person but are ready to take the path of struggle and suffering themselves. Being the supreme manifestation of love and commitment, suffering can provoke a reaction also from those who are imposing the suffering. Thus it becomes transformative of the other too. If we understand suffering in this manner, then we need not fight shy of presenting Jesus as a suffering figure. It will be an occasion of explaining the positive meanings that suffering can have. It is also a different way of looking at God.

In a moment of anger, or more often of fear, people impose suffering on others. But the willing assumption of suffering by the innocent other provokes reflection and leads to change of attitudes. It forces a reexamination of the situation. It breaks the spiral of violence. Here again one person's suffering spares the many from suffering. Such suffering acquires further meaning in the ongoing process of history. It is a stage in the ongoing struggle. It may look like a reverse. But precisely because it provokes reflection, it breaks a cycle; then the consequences and transformation are seen at another level. The struggle may continue, but the situation is no longer one of unilateral oppression. The power of the oppressor is now challenged in an unusual way. A total change may not be achieved immediately. But the process of change has started.

In imposing suffering on another, the person imposing the suffering is treating the other as an object. But the person accepting the suffering without resisting it by counter violence is doing so not passively but under protest, reacting as a free human person. The sufferer refuses to become an object and instead affirms his or her subjectivity. The relationship and the situation are now changed. A new process of interpersonal exchange is started. It makes new hopes possible. Suffering in solidarity with the poor and the oppressed, the hero empowers them to make their own suffering transformative. They become subjects, agents of their own destiny.

This is how a *satyagraha* leads to personal and social transformation. The transformation involves a process and a history. It supposes an open or hidden dialogue—insofar as transformative reflection can be seen as a dialogical response to a challenge.

In the case of Jesus, we may be tempted to see his resurrection as God's response and recompense for his suffering. At a personal level, it is more an approval and confirmation by God than a recompense. At a social level, the experience of the risen Jesus strengthens the disciples and leads them to a renewed commitment to the project of struggle. The *satyagraha* continues. The resurrection, however, is not a solution at the historical level, in which the struggle and the transformation it provokes continue. The resurrection remains a horizon of eschatological hope that enables the disciples to continue the struggle. But it has no immediate or direct impact in the transformation of the people who imposed the suffering. It is a reality and an experience at another level. It is not "pie in the sky" that makes the present suffering bearable. It is not a miraculous solution to the present problem. It is, rather, a symbol of new life possible here and now in this world through personal and social transformation.

Suffering and Kenosis

A calm acceptance of imposed suffering can also be a sign of selflessness. The cause of conflict in the world is egotism, both as selfishness and as pride, which leads one to dominate and exploit others. While one should not run after suffering, a calm acceptance of suffering that is imposed unjustly can be the manifestation of self-gift. When one suffers death, the self-gift is total. Paul sees the acceptance of death on the cross by Jesus as a manifestation of humility and obedience, a total emptying of self:

Do nothing from selfish ambition or conceit, but in humility regard others as better than yourselves. Let each of you look not to your own interests, but to the interests of others. Let the same mind be in you that was in Christ Jesus,
who though he was in the form of God,

did not regard equality with God
as something to be exploited,
but emptied himself,
taking the form of a slave,
being born in human likeness.
And being found in human form,
he humbled himself
and became obedient to the point of death—
even death on a cross. (Phil 2:3–8)

Such emptiness will be filled by God (Phil 2:9–11). But in the meantime the person and the community are transformed. Paul is actually asking the Philippians to "be of the same mind, having the same love, being in full accord and of one mind" (Phil 2:2). A community of peace and love is the goal.

Nonviolence and Dialogue

The preferred nonviolent way of dealing with the other is dialogue. Conversation with the other seeks to provoke, to challenge, to persuade, to convert. It respects the humanity and freedom of the other. It does not impose one's choices because one is convinced of their justice. During his life Jesus dialogues with different kinds of people. There are people like Nicodemus who come as interested inquirers and remain secret admirers and followers from afar (Jn 3:1–21). He explains his mission to John's disciples (Mt 11:2–6). There are others like Nathanael (Jn 1:45–51), the Samaritan woman (Jn 4:1–42), and the Syrophoenician woman (Mk 7:24–30) whom he converts and makes his disciples. There are some, like the Pharisee who invites him for a meal, to whom he patiently explains the situation. A sinful woman comes and washes his feet with her tears, wiping them with her hair. He contrasts the welcome he received from them and shows the link between love and forgiveness (Lk 7:36–50). Similarly he explains his behavior to those who protest against his eating with tax collectors and sinners (Mt 9:10–13; see also Mt 15:1–9). Finally, there are those whom he challenges and condemns, like the Pharisees who protest his plucking grain or healing on the sabbath day (Mt 12:1–14).

The dialogue continues after the resurrection. His dialogue with Mary Magdalene reassures her about his new life and makes her the first apostle of the resurrection (Jn 20:11–18). He dialogues with the two disciples on their way to Emmaus and explains the link between his suffering and his role as the Messiah (Lk 24:13–27). He dialogues with the apostles, particularly the doubting Thomas, to convince them that he is alive and to renew their commission as witnesses to his life, death, and resurrection (Jn 20:19–29). He reaches out to Peter and John on the shores of the lake to confirm his trust in them as leaders (Jn 21:15–23).

Satyagraha and Liberation

With reference to the poor and the oppressed, Jesus is often seen as the liberator. I have used the image of *satyagrahi*. Different images have different focuses, and it is not helpful to compare them. In the Indian tradition the ultimate goal in life is *moksha* or liberation. Therefore Jesus as liberator is leading us to *moksha*. So it is a beautiful image. However, some ideas that are sometimes linked to the image are not helpful. I have already reflected on this earlier. But it may be useful to point them out again.

Some people who see Jesus as liberator consider him a revolutionary. They may even use a passage like Matthew 10:34—"Do not think that I have come to bring peace to the earth; I have not come to bring peace, but a sword"—to justify their stand. Jesus is speaking about preferring God and the kingdom above everything—father and mother, relations, and life itself: "Those who lose their life for my sake will find it" (Mt 10:39). During his arrest, when one of his disciples drew his sword and struck the slave of the high priest, cutting off his ear, Jesus said to him, "Put your sword back into its place; for all who take the sword will perish by the sword" (Mt 26:52). Still, those who see Jesus as a revolutionary would argue that the oppressive socioeconomic and political structures use hidden violence and therefore revolutionary violence against them is justified. It is, of course, questionable whether revolutionary violence has really brought about true liberation and peace anywhere. It seems power only changes hands.

Christians who speak about liberation often refer to the experience of Exodus, when Yahweh frees Israel from their slavery in Egypt and leads them to the promised land. They forget the experience of the exile, where liberation remains an eschatological promise. They ignore the experience of Jesus, whose option for the poor and the oppressed and whose struggle with them for their liberation ends in his death. Jesus, of course, rises again, and we too will share in his resurrection. But it is a trans-historical event. While Jesus identifies himself with the poor, he does not promote socioeconomic or political liberation. He has no blueprint for an ideal society. He is focusing on basic attitudes and relationships like love and forgiveness. He is attacking selfishness, egotism, and pride, which are at the root of all oppression. He certainly wants a new community of freedom, fellowship, and justice. But he wants people to be converted and then build this new society.

Similarly, people who suffer seek to identify themselves with the suffering Jesus. The minjung—the oppressed masses—of Korea look upon Jesus as the minjung. The dalits—the oppressed outcasts—in India see Jesus as a dali. The idea that God in Jesus suffers with them may be a source of comfort and empowerment. But the suffering and death of Jesus lead to the resurrection. They have no meaning without it. Identification with the suffering Jesus has meaning only in such a transformational setting. Suffering for its own sake is not a Christian ideal. Suffering has meaning as an element of protest or as a manifestation of self-giving. Without such meaning, suffering is not a virtue. It has no transformative value. We have to struggle against such meaningless suffering. The cross has liberative value only as an element in a social movement. As such, it is backed up by God's promise of the resurrection. Resurrection as transformation is not a purely otherworldly reality either. It can start now, though its fulfillment may be in the future. Without the resurrection, the cross becomes alienating and humiliating. The cross is often isolated both from the life that led to it and the social movement that followed it, not to speak of the resurrection. On the one hand, one insists rather starkly on the sufferings of Jesus, seen as punishment for the sins of others. The sufferings themselves seem to be glorified, without taking into account the person who suffers and the reasons for which he is suffering. On the other hand, the people who do not like to see Jesus on the cross may not like to see him as the leader and animator of a social movement either. They will be happy to view him as a "soft" guru.

The image of Jesus as *satyagrahi* places the idea of salvation on a personal, human-divine level. It is not something automatic effected by the cross and the sacrifice of Jesus. It is a divine-human interaction marked by freedom on both sides. It is also a social movement promoting both personal and social transformation. The eschatological tension that characterizes it does not make it less historical, though history itself is set in the context of the mystery of God, which transcends history. Jesus calls us to be *satyagrahis* in our turn. He tells us: "If you continue in my word, you are truly my disciples; and you will know the truth, and truth will make you free" (Jn 8:31–32). He also promises us the gift of the Spirit who will guide us into all truth (Jn 16:13).

7

Jesus,
the Avatar

The avatar is a common image in the Indian religious tradition. It is the word used in Indian languages to refer to the incarnation of the Word in Jesus. Roberto de Nobili used it in early seventeenth century. It means descent or manifestation. God is believed to self-manifest in some earthly form to encounter the devotees and grant them liberation. This liberation can be not only personal *(moksha)* but also sociopolitical, that is, liberation from unjust oppressors. Krishna, an avatar of Vishnu, adored as supreme God by one section of Hindus, tells his devotee Arjuna: "For the protection of the good and the destruction of evil, for the purpose of the establishment of dharma, I am born from age to age" *(Bhagavad Gita* 4:8). Ramanuja, commenting on this text, says that an avatar is worthwhile even if it only makes God present to our senses so that we can encounter God in a human way.

In the Indian religious tradition, such manifestations of the divine in history can be many—that is, whenever there is need. The manifestations can take various forms, appropriate to the situation. All avatars are not of the same importance. The devotees of Vishnu, for example, speak of ten avatars. The tenth (final?) one is still to come. Of the other nine, two are considered important and are popular: Rama and Krishna. Rama was a warrior king who vanquished Ravana, presented as an unjust ruler. Krishna guided the good Pandava kings in their battle against the evil Kauravas. We do not have to go into their stories here. Rama is used today by the fundamentalist Hindutva (Hindu identity) movement in India as the symbol of a political liberator, while Krishna is the popular avatar who is loved and worshiped. The point I wish to make here is that avatar is not a univocal concept or category. It can be variously realized at different places at different times.

While the devotees of Vishnu worship him in various avatars, the devotees of Siva think that God cannot become human. But they still believe that Siva can manifest himself in various ways in the lives of his devotees. Siva could have a body, too, though not a human one. He encounters his devotees who are "ripe" for liberation as their guru. Such a guru is a saving figure for the devotee. It is not very clear whether he takes a temporary human form or is simply acting through a living human guru, making him a special mediation. In any case, the devotees of Shiva do not believe in avatars as the devotees of Vishnu do.

My aim here is not to enter into this discussion and try to find a precise meaning for the term avatar in the Hindu (Indian) tradition. Indians looking on Jesus will spontaneously consider him an avatar. It is an Indian religio-cultural entry point to explore our experience of Jesus as a human-divine person. By considering Jesus an avatar my aim is not to compare him with Hindu avatars. I am taking avatar as an image that has a general meaning of "divine manifestation." It implies descent more than ascent. It is not simply the divinization of the human. By looking on Jesus as an avatar, the term *avatar* itself will be taking on a new connotation in the Christian context. Divine manifestations can be many. And yet every manifestation is unique to a particular situation. It is also unique for its particular characteristics. This can be determined only a posteriori. Jesus was experienced by his disciples and others as both human and divine. They saw him as a special avatar, as God incarnate. But this did not exclude for them other divine manifestations in other forms.

The letter to the Hebrews says: "Long ago God spoke to our ancestors in many and various ways by the prophets, but in these last days he has spoken to us by a Son, whom he appointed heir of all things, through whom he also created the worlds" (Heb 1:1–2). Although God speaks through the Son in a special way, God has also spoken through other prophets and in many and various ways. Speaking, of course, is only one form of manifestation focused on the Word. The Spirit of God can be present and manifest herself through the personality, life, and actions of prophetic people. The lives of Moses and John the Baptist were more challenging than their words. We do not hear Mary speak during or after the public life of Jesus. And yet God was a presence in her that animated and guided others. Similarly, we encounter the Divine in holy people. Divine manifestations in this sense are many. They are not always verbal. They are not all of the same kind and importance. We believe that God has not only spoken but is also present and active in a special manner in and through the Son. But this does not exclude other divine manifestations in history.

John, speaking of the Word as light, says: "The true light, which enlightens every one, was coming into the world" (Jn 1:9). An alternate reading of this same text is: "He was the true light that enlightens everyone coming into the world." John goes on to say: "The Word became flesh and lived among us." This means that not only God, but the Word of God too is manifest in various ways.

The *Constitution on the Sacred Liturgy (Sacrosanctum Concilium)* of the Second Vatican Council says:

> To accomplish so great a work Christ is always present in the Church, especially in her liturgical celebrations. He is present in the sacrifice of the Mass not only in the person of his minister, "the same now offering, through the ministry of priests, who formerly offered himself on the cross," but especially in the Eucharistic species. By his power he is present in the sacraments so that when anybody baptizes it is really Christ himself who baptizes. He is present in his word since it is he himself who speaks when the holy scriptures are read in the Church. Lastly he is present when the Church prays and sings, for he has promised "where two or three are gathered together in my name there am I in the midst of them" (Mt 18:20). (*SC*, no. 7)

This document takes for granted God's incarnate manifestation in Jesus Christ and speaks of Christ's other manifestations within the Christian tradition of worship and prayer. Such diversity of presences and manifestations suggests that we should be ready to encounter Jesus in various ways. I think that the term *avatar*, meaning "manifestation," helps us to look at the plurality of manifestations of the Word, of the Spirit, and of God positively and openly and profit from all of them. If we look only at the incarnation of the Word in Jesus, then we may not easily think of other ways in which the Word can also be encountered. It is true that St. Thomas Aquinas says that many incarnations are possible. His reason is that the Word is infinite. Any human nature in which it becomes incarnate can only be finite and limited. So various finite incarnations of the infinite Word are possible.[1] But while from the point of view of revelation many incarnations are possible, from the point of view of salvation we believe that Jesus saved every human, so that no other incarnation is needed. There is only one incarnation in this sense. We need not go into hypothetical issues such as whether there are other universes besides ours or whether there are other races of intelligent beings in other planets of our universe or in other possible universes or whether these intelligent beings need an incarnate savior. Remaining on our own planet, we do not know how salvation reaches out to every human being, even those who do not know and believe in Jesus.

God manifests through the Word and the Spirit in many diverse ways to humans in their history. Acknowledging this plurality of manifestations does not mean that we affirm a priori that all manifestations are the same or that all manifestations are of equal value or significance. We believe in one God. If God chooses to manifest in various ways at various times in various places, these manifestations cannot be chaotic but must be interconnected in some way, called to move toward a convergence. This may have to be discerned a posteriori, given the freedom of God, who manifests, and the freedom of humans, who respond. One of these manifestations is incarnate, and it has to be special. In what this speciality consists, both in itself and with regard to its role in history, also has to be discerned. While all these manifestations are called to interact, they need not be compared and contrasted in an adversarial fashion. They should rather dialogue with one another.

My purpose in talking of Jesus as an avatar is not to evoke all these different manifestations here and see their convergence. This can be done with regard to God's manifestations in the Bible. But with regard to history the process is still open, and the convergence is ongoing. My aim here is rather to see how his disciples see Jesus as a manifestation of the Divine in the human, dense enough to consider it incarnate. But we have to do it in such a way that we do not close the door to other manifestations that may be less dense.

Jesus Is Human

The disciples of Jesus experienced him first of all as a human being like themselves. They seem keen on establishing this. They take steps to specify his historical context. Matthew and Luke provide him with a genealogy that links him not only to his Jewish ancestors but to the first human being (Mt 1:1–17; Lk 3:23–38). Luke further provides a historical context by referring to the political rulers of the time: Herod, the ruler of Judea; the emperor, Augustus; and Quirinius, governor of Syria (Lk 1:5; 2:1–2). Though his birth is attended by miraculous circumstances (Mt 1:18–2:12; Lk 2:8–20), there is no doubt about his being a human child like any other. Joseph had to take him to Egypt to save him from Herod (Mt 2:13–15). Luke tells us clearly, "And Jesus increased in wisdom and in years, and in divine and human favor" (Lk 2:52).

When John the Baptist is preaching and calling people to conversion to prepare for the coming of the Messiah, Jesus too goes to be baptized by John (Mt 3:1–15). Jesus seems to have experienced a special call (Mt 3:16–17) and goes to the desert to prepare himself for his mission with fasting and prayer. He is tempted to usurp power for himself and to use the power given to him for his mission for his own personal benefit and glorification. We have seen these temptations earlier, in Chapter 5. He withstands the temptations (Lk 4:4–12). Luke adds, "When the devil had finished every test, he departed from him until an opportune time" (Lk 4:13). The temptations, therefore, were not a one-time demonstration. When people ask him for a sign (Mt 16:1), even when he is hanging on the cross (Mt 27:42), when they seek to make him king after he feeds five thousand men, besides women and children (Jn 6:15), and when they crowd around him and sing "Hosannah!" as he enters Jerusalem (Mk 11:1–10), Jesus would have been tempted again. When Peter seeks to dissuade him from the suffering he foresees for himself, he tells him curtly, "Get behind me, Satan!" (Mt 16:23). His shrinking from the coming suffering with his prayer to escape it, if possible (Mk 14:32–42), and his cry on the cross "My God, my God, why have you forsaken me?" (Mk 15:34) were the final moments of this ongoing process of temptations. They are also moments for his total submission to the will of God, his Father. We can therefore understand when the letter to the Hebrews says, "We do not have a high priest who is unable to sympathize with our weaknesses, but we have one who in every respect has been tested as we are, yet without sin" (Heb 4:15).

In relating to others, Jesus shows normal human reactions. He loves to have little children around him. He must have played with them. He is indignant with his disciples for stopping them. He holds them up as models for people who receive the kingdom of God. "He took them up in his arms, laid his hands on them and blessed them" (Mk 10:13–16). He yields before the persistence and repartee of the Canaanite woman. She is asking him to cure her daughter. When Jesus tells her that his mission is restricted to the Jews and that "it is not fair to take the children's food and throw it to the dogs," she retorts, "Yes, Lord, yet even the dogs eat the crumbs that fall from their masters' table." Then Jesus answers: "Woman, great is your faith! Let it be done for you as you wish" (Mt 15:21–28). When a rich young man comes to ask him, "Good Teacher, what I must do to inherit eternal life?" Mark tells us that Jesus, "looking at him, loved him and said, 'Go, sell everything, give to the poor and then come and follow me.'" The young man does not follow Jesus because he had many possessions (Mk 10:17–22). Similarly, Jesus loves Lazarus of Bethany (Jn 11:3) and weeps as he stands before his tomb (Jn 11:35), even though he raises him to life after that. He laments over Jerusalem and its coming destruction because the Jews would not be converted (Mt 23:37–39; Lk 19:41–44).

He is disappointed that his "chosen" disciples are not able to watch and pray with him even as he is sweating blood. He asks them, "Could you not stay awake with me one hour?" (Mt 26:40; Lk 22:44). He angrily drives away the buyers and sellers in the Temple for turning it from a house of prayer to a den of robbers (Mt 21:12–13). He denounces the Pharisees and scribes in no uncertain terms for misleading and exploiting the people. He accuses them of hypocrisy, casuistry, love of honor, and blindness (Mt 23:1–36). Jesus, of course, is most human and vulnerable when he is betrayed, suffers, and dies on the cross, abandoned by every one (Mt 26:47–56).

Jesus is also very human in the way he deals with the people. He goes out to the poor and suffering. When a great crowd follows him into the desert, we are told that "he had compassion for them, because they were like sheep without a shepherd; and he began to teach them many things" (Mk 6:34). Matthew adds, "He cured their sick" (Mt 14:14). He does not accept the suggestion of the disciples to send them away so that they can find food in the villages around; rather, he opts to feed them (Mk 6:35–44). The image of people crowding around him is evoked frequently in the gospels (Mt 4:23–25; 8:18). He is particularly sensitive to the poor, the oppressed, and the marginalized—the tax collectors and sinners (Mt 9:10–13). He reaches out to the Samaritan woman, doubly oppressed as woman and as a Samaritan, and makes her and, through her, the whole village his disciples (Jn 4:1–42). He visits the house of Zacchaeus the tax collector, whose desire to see Jesus makes him climb a tree (Lk 19:1–10). He praises the widow who put two small copper coins into the Temple treasury (Lk 20:2). He protects the sinful woman who washes his feet with her tears and wipes them with her hair (Lk 7:36–50) and the woman taken in adultery, whom the Jews wanted to stone to death (Jn 8:1–11). He holds up the good Samaritan as a model of brotherly love (Lk 10:25–37) and the humble tax collector as an example of sincere prayer (Lk 18:9–14).

Jesus had friends like Martha, Mary, and Lazarus, whose company he enjoyed (Lk 10:38–42; Jn 11:1–44). He did not discriminate against women. He had women disciples, who not only followed him but also provided for his needs (Lk 8:1–3). Some women disciples follow him on his way to the cross and to the tomb and are the first to search for him and encounter him on the third day when he is risen (Lk 23:27–31; Mt 27:55–56, 61; 28:1–10; Jn 20:11–18). Jesus did not shun invitations from the Pharisees either, using such opportunities to dialogue with them and challenge them. It is in a Pharisee's house that he explains the link between love and forgiveness on the occasion of a sinful woman washing his feet with her tears (Lk 7:36–50). He compares her love with the "coolness" with which the Pharisee received him. He gives life to the daughter of Jairus, a leader of the synagogue. The people whose faith he openly praises are mostly Gentiles or non-Jews: the centurion whose servant he heals (Lk 7:1–10), the Canaanite woman (Mk 7:24–30), and the Samaritan woman (Jn 4:1–42).

Jesus Is Divine

The disciples of Jesus and others certainly saw Jesus as a rabbi or teacher and a prophet who proclaimed the kingdom of God and called people to conversion. But a closer look at his deeds and words seems to point to a deeper dimension of his personality. First of all, he speaks with special authority. Unlike the other prophets who spoke in the name of God, Jesus speaks in his own name. "You have heard that it was said . . . But *I* say to you . . . " (Mt 5:21). With this authority Jesus makes some radical proposals, unlike the rabbis who only interpret the law. He not only insists on right intentions and attitudes rather than mere external and behavioral conformity to the law, but he demands love for enemies and suggests that one should turn the other cheek when one is struck (Mt 5:38–48). He does not encourage practices like easy divorce. He suggests that the husband and wife, made in the image of God, "are no longer two, but one flesh. Therefore what God has joined together, let no one separate . . . Whoever divorces his wife, except for unchastity, and marries another commits adultery." When the disciples say that then it is better not to marry, he proposes to them the ideal of celibacy "for the sake of the kingdom" (Mt 19:1–12). He demands radical commitment that may go against family ties, suggesting that whoever loves father or mother, son or daughter "more than me is not worthy of me" (Mt 10:34–39). He demands radical reversal: "Those who want to save their life will lose it, and those who lose their life for my sake will find it" (Mt 16:25). He praises poverty and humility (Mt 5:3–12; 11:25–30). He challenges their laws of purity and pollution (Mt 15:10–20). He eats with the ritually polluted tax collectors and sinners (Mt 9:10–13). He defies their interpretation of the sabbath and claims the authority to reinterpret it, enunciating the basic principle that the sabbath is for humans and not humans for the sabbath (Mt 12:1–14; Jn 5:1–18).

He sets his work in an eschatological context. In the synagogue at Nazareth he reads from Isaiah:

> "The Spirit of the Lord is upon me,
>   because he has anointed me to bring the good news to
>   the poor.
> He has sent me to proclaim release to the captives
>   and recovery of sight to the blind,
>   to let the oppressed go free,
> to proclaim the year of the Lord's favor." (Lk 4:18–19)

Then he announces: "Today this scripture has been fulfilled in your hearing" (Lk 4:21).

His miracles of healing and exorcism are the symbolic arrival of the kingdom of God. Obviously, he does not aim at healing every sick person in Palestine. But his works manifest the presence of the healing power of God. The healing itself is only a sign of forgiveness and reconciliation. He presents the image of a forgiving God (Lk 15) and exhorts the disciples to forgive one another (Mt 6:12; 18:21–22). He himself claims authority to forgive sins, though God alone can forgive sins, as the scribes point out (Mt 9:2–8). When he asks the disciples, "Who do people say the Son of man is?" (Mt 16:13),

Peter confesses him to be the messiah. However, Jesus himself does not seem to stress this title too much since people were expecting a political messiah, one who would reestablish the kingdom of Israel. But when he is accused of claiming to be the messiah or the king of the Jews at his trial before the Jewish leaders and Pilate, he does not deny it, though he specifies that his is not an earthly kingdom (Mk 14:53–65; Jn 18:28–38).

Jesus is called the Son of God in some passages in the gospels (Mt 16:16–17; Mk 14:61–62). He claims a special relationship to God, whom he calls his Father, with the specially endearing name Abba (Mt 26:39). But he shares this relationship with the disciples, since they too feel free to call God Abba (Gal 4:6; Rom 8:15). However, he seems to make a distinction between himself and his disciples when he says, "I am ascending to my Father and your Father" (Jn 20:17). In John's gospel he describes himself as God's "only Son" (Jn 3:16). He also says, "The Father and I are one" and "Whoever has seen me has seen the Father," though exegetes generally say that this unity is functional. "If I am not doing the works of my Father, then do not believe me. But if I do them, even though you do not believe me, believe the works, so that you may know and understand that the Father is in me and I am in the Father" (Jn 10:37–38). He says further, "No one knows the Son except the Father, and no one knows the Father except the Son and anyone to whom the Son chooses to reveal him" (Mt 11:27; Lk 10:22). All these passages affirm a special relationship between Jesus and God. Some of his miracles, like calming the stormy sea (Mk 4:35–41) and restoring the dead to life (Mk 5:21–24, 35–43; Lk 7:11–17; Jn 11:38–44), show that he is more than an ordinary worker of miracles. These miracles cannot be explained psychologically.

He often refers to himself as the Son of man. This probably refers to Daniel 7:13, which talks about "one like a son of man" coming with the clouds of heaven. With this title Jesus may be presenting himself as an eschatological judge (Mt 24:29–31; 25:31; 26:64). He does so also before the high priest who asks him, "Are you the Messiah?" Jesus answers, "I am; and you will see the Son of man seated at the right hand of the Power, and coming with the clouds of heaven" (Mk 14:61–62). His presence and action call for a decision. To accept him is to accept God; to reject him is to reject God (Mt 21:33–46). Jesus tells his disciples: "I am the way, and the truth, and the life. No one comes to the Father except through me. If you know me, you will know my Father also . . . The words that I say to you I do not speak on my own; but the Father who dwells in me does his works. Believe me that I am in the Father and the Father is in me" (Jn 14:6–7, 10–11). Jesus goes on to say, "The one who believes in me will also do the works that I do and, in fact, will do greater works than these" (Jn 14:12). This means that Jesus shares with us his own filial relationship with the Father.

For the disciples, the resurrection of Jesus confirms that he is the messiah. They also realize that he is a different kind of messiah than the one that the Jews were expecting. He is not going to establish an earthly kingdom. They feel sent to proclaim and build up the kingdom that this messiah has inaugurated, which is a new community in which people love and serve each other (Mk 16:9–20; Mt 28; Jn 20:19–23; Acts 2:14–36). And they are waiting for the second coming of Jesus, when the kingdom of God will be definitely established. After the ascension of Jesus the angel tells the disciples, "This Jesus, who has been taken up from you into heaven, will come in the same way as you saw him go into heaven" (Acts 1:11). They enter into a period of "already—not yet." The presence and work of Jesus in the world is not over. It continues. Jesus had promised the disciples, "I am with you always, to the end of the age" (Mt 28:20). The disciples felt that the "Lord worked with them" (Mk 16:20). His presence is assured particularly by the gift of the Holy Spirit (Jn 15:26; Acts 2:1–13). But they have to play their role in that context.

A Cosmic Dimension

The work of Jesus transcends his own lifetime on this earth, acquiring cosmic dimensions. Paul has this cosmic vision. But he attributes the work variously to the Father, to Christ, or to the Spirit. To the Ephesians he writes:

Blessed be the God and Father of our Lord Jesus Christ, who has blessed us in Christ with every spiritual blessing in the heavenly places, just as he chose us in Christ before the foundation of the world to be holy and blameless before him in love. He destined us for adoption as his children through Jesus Christ, according to the good pleasure of his will, to the praise of his glorious grace that he freely bestowed on us in the Beloved. In him we have redemption through his blood, the forgiveness of his trespasses, according to the riches of his grace that he lavished on us. With all wisdom and insight he has made known to us the mystery of his will, according to his good pleasure that he set forth in Christ, as a plan for the fullness of time, to gather up all things in him, things in heaven and things on earth. (Eph 1:3–10)

To the Corinthians he speaks of Christ as firstfruits, subjecting everything to the Father: "When all things are subjected to him, then the Son himself will also be subjected to the one who put all things in subjection to him, so that God may be all in all" (1 Cor 15:28). In his letter to the Romans, Paul speaks of the Spirit:

If the Spirit of him who raised Jesus from the dead dwells in you, he who raised Christ from the dead will give life to your mortal bodies also through his Spirit that dwells in you . . . For all who are led by the Spirit of God are children of God. For you did not receive a spirit of slavery to fall back into fear, but you have received a spirit of adoption. When we cry "Abba! Father!" it is that very Spirit bearing witness with our spirit that we are children of God, and if children, then heirs, heirs of God and joint heirs with Christ—if, in fact, we suffer with him so that we may also be glorified with him . . .

For the creation waits with eager longing for the revealing of the children of God . . . We know that the whole creation has been groaning in labor pains until now; and not only creation, but we ourselves, who have the firstfruits of the Spirit, groan inwardly while we wait for adoption, the redemption of our bodies. (Rom 8:11, 15–17, 19, 22–23)

We see that Paul's theological reading of history is a complex one involving the Father, Christ, and the Spirit. In the life of Jesus he sees a "descending-ascending" pattern. He speaks of Christ Jesus

> Who, though he was in the form of God,
>   did not regard equality with God as something to be
>   exploited,
> but emptied himself, taking the form of a slave,
>   being born in human likeness.
> And being found in human form,
>   he humbled himself and became obedient to the point
>   of death—
> even death on a cross.
>
> Therefore God also highly exalted him
>   and gave him the name that is above every name,
> so that at the name of Jesus every knee should bend,
>   in heaven and on earth and under the earth,
> and every tongue should confess
>   that Jesus Christ is Lord, to the glory of God the
>   Father. (Phil 2:5–11)

John presents another cosmic vision focused on Jesus as the Word of God:

In the beginning was the Word and the Word was with God, and the Word was God. He was in the beginning with God. All things came into being through him, and without him not one thing came into being. What has come into being was life, and the life was the light of all people . . . The true light, which enlightens every one, was coming into the world . . . To all who received him, who believed in his name, he gave power to become children of God . . . And the Word became flesh and lived among us . . . From his fullness we have all received, grace upon grace. (Jn 1:1–5, 9, 12, 14, 16)

John will complete this story that starts at the beginning with a vision of the end: "That they may all be one. As you, Father, are in me and I am in you, may they also be in us, so that the world may believe that you have sent me. The glory that you have given me I have given them, so that they may be one as we are one" (Jn 17:21–22).

What is clear from these meditations of Paul and John is that the work of Jesus is set in the context of the work of the Father and of the Spirit. This is the root of his double identity. He is divine, but he is God in communion with the Father and the Spirit. But he is also with us in history, human. His work encompasses the whole of history. It is still going on.

Jesus is therefore seen as human and divine. Jesus is a man. But in him the disciples encounter God. They do not perceive Jesus as divine straight away. They experience God present and active in him. Knowing him one knows God. He forgives sins and gives us a share in divine life. He makes us children of God, sharing with us his own sonship. He can do this only because he is divine—God. But *god* is not a univocal term that we can apply equally without qualification to the Father, Son, and Spirit. So to say simply that Jesus is God would be misleading. He himself would not have claimed that. He spoke of his Father. He is the mediator (Heb 8) of a new covenant between God and humanity. The early Christians also pray to him as God. We only have to recall the apostle Thomas's acclamation: "My Lord and my God!" (Jn 20:28). There is a complexity here and a polarity. They have to be kept in balance and tension. It is not easy.

The Compromise of Chalcedon

Problems started when this complex reality of Jesus and its awareness entered the Greek intellectual world. The Greeks operated with clear and distinct concepts. Terms like *god* and *man* had clear definitions. They were normally incompatible. God is infinite, eternal, and almighty. Man, on the other hand, is finite, weak, and destined for death. It is not easy to reconcile them. Faced with a divine-human like Jesus, they tended to emphasize one pole or the other. Some stress that Jesus is God. Then he cannot really be a human being. He can only put on an appearance of being human. Others insist that he is man. He can only be a creature, even if he is considered the best—the "firstborn." It is not necessary for us here to go into the technical terms of these discussions. After a lengthy process of argumentation a special group irons out a compromise formulation that says that he is one person in two natures, "consubstantial" (of the same substance) both with God and with humans. These should be neither separated nor confused. In nontechnical language this is to say that Jesus is both divine and human, God and man.

Different groups in the church interpreted the compromise document differently. In the Latin church the tendency has been to emphasize the divinity of Jesus Christ. It is the divine person who takes on a human nature. The humanity of Jesus has been slowly downplayed in practice. Jesus is simply worshiped as God, especially in popular religiosity, though most of the official prayers are addressed to the Father through Jesus Christ.

Contemporary attempts at rediscovering the humanity of Jesus often err in the other direction. Jesus becomes so human that one does not see how his being God has any meaning. Once created, the world is self-sufficient. It does not need God. The world is seen as an automatic machine. God is seen as the one who brought it into being and set it moving. But once the machine is moving, the mover becomes irrelevant. So God is no longer needed. This is the process of secularization. To speak of Jesus Christ as divine or God sounds dissonant in this paradigm. Some, however, see Jesus as a human being specially possessed and animated by the Spirit of God.

Jesus, the Avatar

I think that the Indian approach can escape the Greek dichotomous one that separates God from the human and then does not know how to put them together. This is not to say that it would find it easier to understand and explain the mystery of Jesus Christ, the divine-human. But it would look at it differently. First of all, both the Shivites and the Vaishnavites accept the possibility that God has a body, without detriment to his infinite qualities. The Vaishnavites further believe that God can take on a human body. On the one hand, God is not so distant and separate from the world and humans that no real link is possible. On the other hand, God is not present in the world in such a way that everything is somehow divine. This would be pantheistic. The idea of the avatar affirms the possibility that God can choose to manifest in and through the world and humans in various ways. God can become human and reach out to humans in a human way. God becoming human is not a humiliation or imperfection. It is not unthinkable that God can become present in history as a human. The tradition of avatars testifies to this.

Though God's avatars can be many, we Christians believe that Jesus Christ is an avatar like no other—incarnational. Besides this specificity, this avatar is further characterized by three factors, among many others. God in Jesus Christ does not come in power and majesty but comes emptying himself as a suffering servant, giving us an example of self-giving love. Therefore, the specificity of the incarnation does not display itself in a visibly striking manner. Second, the humanity that God takes on in Jesus Christ does not disappear with his death but endures in history and eternity. Third, Jesus Christ is in solidarity with the whole of humanity and the whole cosmos, leading it to final fulfillment. What is important here is fidelity to our experience of Jesus Christ in faith, not to an intellectual framework, Greek or Indian. Rational elaboration is not a deepening but an impoverishment of the living experience of God, who can be touched and loved as a human being in Jesus. The Greek tradition, particularly, by reducing the divine and the human to essences—"nature"—loses the density of the divine and the human and their mutual ongoing interaction. It does not concentrate on the historical concreteness—the life and the activities—of the human. I think that the term avatar keeps the divine-human tension alive.[2]

The humanity of Jesus has not disappeared with his death. It is still there, though he is risen. Jesus can be loved as a human being even today. The divine-human tension in Jesus is very much alive. Jesus is still Emmanuel—God with us. Jesus is an avatar, in descent. Once he has become human, the re-ascent involves the integration of the human with the Divine. God now has a body, even if it is a risen body. The tension between the divine and the human in Jesus is not static but dynamic, because it is a history. The humanity of Jesus does not disappear from history after the resurrection. Rather, it continues to mediate the divine in the eschatological period of the already and not yet. The integration between the divine and human in Jesus and the divine and the humans in the world will be complete only on the last day. The humanity of Jesus has not only a personal but a corporate role. This is indicated by the symbols like the vine and the branches (Jn 15:1–6) and the church (humanity) as the body of Christ (1 Cor 12:12–31). In this way the historical process becomes integral to the avatar.

We also realize that history itself has a double dimension. There is what we normally consider history conditioned by space, time, and movement—before and after, in a horizontal sense. Underlying this or transcending this, depending on which spatial metaphor one wants to use, there is another level of reality that is not simply the eternity of God, usually described by theologians as *tota simul* (everything at the same time). There is a dimension that transcends time but is not eternity. It corresponds to the spirit in humans. It has a history too—a before and an after. But there is also a simultaneity. When I love another person, my love is not conditioned by time and space.

It transcends them in a way. Yet it can grow and change. It expresses itself through a succession of gestures—words and actions. It transcends them, though it cannot be real without them. This is the reality of the spirit and its corporal dimension.

I feel that the one person–two natures paradigm, while it is true, simplifies and makes abstract a complex and tensive reality. It is metaphysical and transcendental. It does not focus on the concrete, historical way in which the divine and the human in Jesus interact and evolve. It does not make space for other real manifestations of the Divine, though they may not have the same density. A focus on the image of the avatar can help us to recover the complexity and the tension. It seems easy to experience the humanity of God and relate to it in a human way. The dispute between the Arians and the Nestorians may not have happened in India, since God becoming human would not have been seen as an impossibility. I think that the devotion in India around the avatar is much more alive and responsive to this complexity. There is an effort to remember and participate in the human life of the avatar that we see in Europe only in some mystics like Francis of Assisi and Ignatius of Loyola.

God is always relating to us as God (Father), Word, and Spirit. This is from creation. But in Jesus, God reaches out to us in a historical, human way. In and through Jesus we encounter God in a human way. Indian devotional tradition imaginatively exploits all the human relationships and emotions in reaching out to the avatar of God. Krishna, for instance, is imagined as mother, child, servant, bridegroom, and bride by the Tamil poet Bharathi. The point is that God in the avatar is relating to us in a human way. Christians are very hesitant to explore these devotional ways. When they go beyond concentration on the passion of Jesus, they focus on him mostly as a child and as a bridegroom. At Christmas time one sings lullabies to baby Jesus. Mystics speak of Jesus as their bridegroom. But this is not common among ordinary devotees. It is more common today to look on Jesus as a brother. Sometimes Jesus is also looked on as a friend. Did not Jesus say, "I do not call you servants any longer, but I have called you friends" (Jn 15:15)? The self-emptying image of Jesus proposed by Paul to the Philippians (Phil 2:1–11) and the picture of Jesus washing the feet of the disciples (Jn 13:1–20) can lead us to look on Jesus as servant. Going beyond these obvious images some have related to Jesus as mother. This is interesting because it crosses the gender barrier. For instance, the poet Narayan Vaman Tilak (1862–1919) sings:

Tenderest Mother-Guru mine,
Saviour, where is love like thine?[3]

Tilak also explore other human relationships, such as Jesus as lord and beloved: "Lord Jesus Christ, Beloved, tell, O tell me true, what shall Thy servant do?"[4] Here are a whole series of images:

> As the moon and its beams are one,
>   So, that I be one with Thee,
> This is my prayer to Thee, my Lord,
>   This is my beggar's plea.
> I would snare Thee and hold Thee ever
>   In loving, wifely ways;
> I give Thee a daughter's welcome,
>   I give Thee a sister's praise.
> Take this being, O my Christ,
>   Dwell as its soul within.[5]

The problem is that, apart from an occasional poem or hymn, such relationships are not part of popular devotion. People rarely go beyond looking on Jesus as Lord and God. This means that their attention remains focused on his divinity. His humanity is on the margins, if not forgotten. A rediscovery of the humanity of Jesus will lead us to explore all these different relationships. The arts, especially music and dance, can explore all these relationships and lead devotees to ecstasy.

But in Christianity there is another, very specific manifestation. That is the manifestation of Jesus in the poor. Jesus blesses people for giving him food, clothing, comfort, and so on. When people ask him when they did this, he answers, "Just as you did it to one of the least of these who are members of the family, you did it to me" (Mt 25:40).

Jesus as Symbol of God?

Many years ago Edward Schillebeeckx wrote about Jesus as the sacrament of our encounter with God. It is the experience of God in Jesus that leads us to realize that God is not a simple unity. We do not know what God is in God's interior being. God is certainly beyond "name and form," as the Indian tradition would say. All that we can really say about God is that God is not this, not this *(neti, neti)*. We have an apophatic tradition also in Christianity. We do not understand fully who or what God is. We can only reflect on our own experience, which is conditioned both by what God chooses to manifest to us and by our own limitations, by our culture and history. Without going into the metaphysics of concepts like *person* and *nature*, we can say that we experience God in various ways as Father, Jesus, and Spirit. God manifests Godself in various ways.

Some people today speak of Jesus as the symbol of God. When we say that Jesus is the symbol of God, we fall into the trap of the opposing terms: *symbol-real*. Karl Rahner speaks of "real-symbol." But it is a conceptual category. Either Jesus is really God or he is only a symbol of God. Such a dichotomy is deceiving. Jesus is not simply God, who is Father, Son, and Spirit. But we encounter God in and through Jesus. God in Jesus acts in a human way as a human being in history. We see Jesus as the Word incarnate. There are two dimensions to God's activity in Jesus. The human dimension is the symbol or manifestation or sensible (meaning "of the senses") and historical expression of the Divine. In the same way, we can say that the body is the symbol of the spirit in the human. I love a person. My love is a composite spirit-body action. Insofar as it is the spirit's action, it is not really limited by the material factors of the body and of space and time. But when it takes bodily form, it has to be in space and time and go through a historical process. Even verbalizing my love has to be done somewhere, at some time, over a period of time. My love becomes fully human only when I express it also bodily. And yet what I do or express bodily is the symbol of what I am doing or experiencing as spirit. My experience of love at the level of the spirit may find expression in a multiplicity of successive manifestations. It becomes a story.

We can reflect analogically on the Word and Jesus. The Word becomes historically present and active in Jesus. The Word of God does not become active only with the birth of Jesus. As John says, the Word was from the beginning, creating and enlightening everything. Then the Word becomes flesh and enters into history as Jesus. What Jesus does is the human, bodily expression in space, time, and history of what the Word does. Of course, Jesus does not give human, bodily expression to all that the Word does. But what Jesus does is the manifestation of the Word, and through the Word, of God. This is what we wish to indicate by saying that Jesus is the symbol of God. But the term *symbol* may be inadequate and lead to confusion, because it is used in many other contexts with less dense and complex meanings.

That is why I think that the term *avatar* may help. I am not saying that *avatar* has this meaning in the Indian theological tradition. I am saying that it can be given this new meaning in the Christian context. It stands for the Divine in the human or the Divine that we can touch in the human. On the one hand, we cannot touch the Divine in the same way outside the avatar. On the other hand, the Divine can intervene in history in this particular manner only through the avatar. There are no abstract "meanings" that can be expressed in various ways. These are concrete meanings that can be expressed only in this way and in no other. Other concrete expressions are possible. But every concrete expression has a uniqueness that is particular to it. In a way the term *symbol* may not be indicative of this particularity. People can say "Oh! It is only a symbol" or "Oh! It is only one among many symbols." The avatar is not just a symbol. It is a historical manifestation, particularized and consequently limited by concrete historical circumstances. This is true even of the incarnate manifestation that is subject to the limitations of its human nature.

The uniqueness of Jesus, according to Christian belief, depends not so much on his incarnational manifestation but on the paschal mystery. As I mentioned earlier, Thomas Aquinas did not see any problem with the possibility of many incarnations, since an incarnation is only a limited manifestation of the Infinite. But he would not have found many paschal mysteries meaningful. The birth and human activity of Jesus before death were limited to Palestine. He was culturally and historically limited. But the liberating and life-giving love that he lived out in his passion, death, and resurrection reached out to the whole of humanity. At the level of history this universal inclusion takes the form of the eschatological movement that we call the church. The church, again, is only a symbol and servant—a sacrament—of the plan of God that is being realized progressively till the whole universe is free (Rom 8) and united (Eph 1:10) and God is "all in all" (1 Cor 15:28).

Today we realize that God's presence and action are not limited to the church. God can self-manifest in various ways to various peoples. This does not mean that God's manifestations are all the same or equal. But all of them have the same goal—God's reign. Christians believe that the paschal mystery of Jesus is central to this cosmic process, though they would not know how to explain it or even understand fully the process of it. I think that the basis for this affirmation is that Jesus is divine. But this does not exclude a plurality of divine manifestations and mediations, though they are all seen as participative in the one project of God in Christ and the Spirit. If the Spirit of God and of Christ is present and active in other religions, this presence will have to be manifested in some historical way through persons and events. These are all manifestations or avatars of God, of the Word, and of the Spirit. This is why Jesus as avatar seems a more inclusive image, though he is a special avatar. It is true to say that there are many avatars and that Jesus is a special incarnate avatar. But we cannot say that there are many incarnations and Jesus is a special one. Avatar is a more inclusive category than incarnation.

The privileged place to encounter Jesus as avatar is obviously the New Testament. The New Testament image of Jesus will also give us one of the criteria to judge the authenticity of other manifestations. They cannot be contradictory, though they can be different and convergent. Faced with such a diversity of manifestations, an attitude of dialogue and openness seems the appropriate way to facilitate their convergence.

8

Jesus, the Servant

A Buddhist monk in Sri Lanka seeking to portray Jesus chose the image of him washing the feet of his disciples. The artist's choice is significant. As a matter of fact, reading through the gospels, apart from the image of Jesus hanging on the cross, it is the most striking image. John tells us the story:

> During supper Jesus, knowing that the Father had given all things into his hands, and that he had come from God and was going to God, got up from the table, took off his outer robe, and tied a towel around himself. Then he poured water into a basin and began to wash the disciples' feet and to wipe them with the towel that was tied around him . . . After he had washed their feet, had put on his robe, and had returned to the table, he said to them, "Do you know what I have done to you? You call me Teacher and Lord—and you are right, for that is what I am. So if I, your Lord and Teacher, have washed your feet, you also ought to wash one another's feet. For I have set you an example, that you also should do as I have done to you." (Jn 13:3–5; 12–15)

A Moral Ideal

This gesture of Jesus can be taken as a moral exhortation in action. Jesus offers himself as a model of humility. We can recall the teachings of Jesus in this context. Matthew tells the story:

> At that time the disciples came to Jesus and asked, "Who is the greatest in the kingdom of heaven?" He called a child, whom he put among them, and said, "Truly I tell you, unless you change and become like children, you will never enter the kingdom of heaven. Whoever becomes

122

humble like this child is the greatest in the kingdom of heaven. Whoever welcomes one such child in my name welcomes me." (Mt 18:1–5)

Mark and Luke indicate that the question of the disciples was not an innocent one. As a matter of fact, they were disputing among themselves, asking who among them was the greatest (Mk 9:33–37; Lk 9:46–48). Jesus seems to set his teaching in the context of the Pharisees seeking respect and honor in public places. He suggests a different way of life:

"Call no one your father on earth, for you have one Father—the one in heaven. Nor are you to be called instructors, for you have one instructor, the Messiah. The greatest among you will be your servant. All who exalt themselves will be humbled, and all who humble themselves will be exalted." (Mt 23:9–12)

This is the reason that Jesus pronounces blessedness on the poor and the meek and the persecuted (Mt 5:1–12). Mary's song of praise emphasizes the same point:

"He has brought down the powerful from their thrones,
    and lifted the lowly;
he has filled the hungry with good things,
    and sent the rich away empty." (Lk 1:52–53)

No wonder, then, that Jesus invites his disciples to "take my yoke upon you, and learn from me; for I am gentle and humble in heart" (Mt 11:29).

From Morality to Spirituality

This exhortation to humility can be understood from the moral point of view. Jesus opposes this attitude to that of the Pharisees, who are proud and self-sufficient. Humility is truth. Acceptance of this truth makes it a spiritual affirmation. Whatever we have is God's gift to us. We are nothing on our own. Since everything is God's gift, when we accept our emptiness, God fills us. It is in this context that we discover that the action of Jesus is not just a modeling of his teaching. It is the essence of his life. Humility in the form of self-emptying becomes his very way of being, his existence. Paul illustrates this passage from humility in the moral sense to self-emptying in a spiritual sense. He exhorts the Philippians:

Do nothing from selfish ambition or conceit, but in humility regard others as better than yourselves. Let each of you look not to your own

interests, but to the interest of others. Let the same mind be in you that
was in Christ Jesus,

> who, though he was in the form of God,
>> did not regard equality with God
>> as something to be exploited,
> but emptied himself,
>> taking the form of a slave,
>> being born in human likeness.
> And being found in human form,
>> he humbled himself
>> and became obedient to the point of death—
> even death on a cross.
>
> Therefore God also highly exalted him
>> and gave him the name
>> that is above every name,
> so that at the name of Jesus
>> every knee should bend,
>> in heaven and on earth and under the earth,
> and every tongue should confess
>> that Jesus Christ is Lord,
>> to the glory of God the Father. (Phil 2:3–11)

For Jesus, becoming humble is not simply an element of moral behavior but
a way of life. Actually it is more than a way of life; it is a way of salvation.
God makes all of us pass with Jesus through death to life. Jesus is the
firstfruits. Jesus makes this passage in solidarity with humanity. Paul tells the
Romans:

> Do you not know that all of us who have been baptized into Christ
> Jesus were baptized into his death? Therefore we have been buried with
> him by baptism into death, so that, just as Christ was raised from the
> dead by the glory of the Father, so we too might walk in newness of
> life. (Rom 6:3–4)

So when Jesus dies and rises again, all of us die and rise with him. The self-
emptying and exaltation of Jesus become a process of salvation for all beings.

The self-emptying of Jesus has sometimes been explained in a moral sense
as well. The humble obedience of Jesus is contrasted with the proud disobe-
dience of Adam and Eve. The humility of Jesus "makes up" for the pride of

Adam and Eve. Humility is no longer an element of moral behavior. It is deepened into an element of the process of salvation itself.

Self-emptying and Fruitfulness

I think that Jesus, in his teaching and in his life, deepens this mystery further. Dying and rising is not a special process of salvation. It is the process of life itself. It is the cosmic process:

"Unless a grain of wheat falls into the earth and dies, it remains just a single grain; but if it dies, it bears much fruit. Those who love their lives lose it, and those who hate their life in this world will keep it for eternal life." (Jn 12:24–25)

Death is not merely the way to new and fuller life. It is also the condition of fruitfulness in abundance. Our proper attitude to life is not to hold on to it, but to surrender it, offer it. From this gift new life emerges for oneself and for others. Life is a gift. We receive it as a gift and make of it a gift to others, then we receive it again in a different form. To be empty is to be full. To die is to live. In one sense this is the cosmic process: death assures the continuity of life in different forms. Death is not a loss but a transformation. This can happen at any time. Paul experienced this:

I have been crucified with Christ; and it is no longer I who live, but it is Christ who lives in me. And the life I now live in the flesh I live by faith in the Son of God, who loved me and gave himself for me. (Gal 2:19–20)

This is the mystery. I give up my life. I empty myself. Jesus responds by emptying himself and becoming a gift to me. Now Jesus lives in me. This is a process of mutual emptying that leads to fullness. It is death leading to life. That is why Jesus says, "Unless a grain of wheat falls into the earth and dies, it remains just a single grain; but if it dies, it bears much fruit" (Jn 12:24).

Jesus sets his own death in such a context. His attempt to explain it to his disciples may not have had much success. When Peter confesses him to be the Messiah, he does not deny it, but he adds that

"the Son of Man must undergo great suffering, and be rejected by the elders, chief priests, and scribes, and be killed, and on the third day be raised." (Lk 9:22)

Jesus goes on to suggest that this is the way for everyone:

> Then he said to them all, "If any want to become my followers, let them deny themselves and take up their cross daily and follow me. For those who want to save their lives will lose it, and those who lose their life for my sake will save it." (Lk 9:29)

Jesus will come back to this even after his resurrection, when he explains this mystery to the disciples who are on their way to Emmaus (Lk 24:26).

It may be time now to stop a little and look back on the way that we have made. Normally, people in the world tend to be proud of what they are, what they have, and what they do. They boast, are self-righteous, and demand respect from others. They seek to dominate others, throw about their weight, so to speak. The Jewish leaders did so. The Pharisees based their claims on their faithful observance of the law. They looked down on everyone else. In this context, to see Jesus—whom everyone considered a rabbi, a teacher—wash the feet of his disciples was a great example of humility. Jesus is the opposite of the Jewish leaders. But the servanthood of Jesus is more than a simple moral principle of good behavior. Humility is self-emptying. Self-emptying is self-gift. Total self-gift can take the form of death. But such death leads to life—new and fuller life. Through servanthood Jesus leads us to the deeper mysteries of life and death. But this mysterious dimension supposes that death itself need not be physical. It can very well be lived as humble, self-giving service to the other. Thus we come a full circle. Service becomes the symbol of death and life. To say that Jesus is servant is to say that he is the savior, the life-giver.

The Suffering Servant of Yahweh

In Isaiah there is a figure called the servant of Yahweh (Is 42:1–7; 49:1–6; 50:4–9; 52:13–53:12). He is also known as the suffering servant. I think that the suffering servant of Yahweh and Jesus as servant throw light on each other. Therefore it is worth meditating on the song of the suffering servant.

> See my servant shall prosper;
>   he shall be exalted and lifted up,
>   and shall be very high.
> Just as there were many who were astonished at him—
>   so marred was his appearance, beyond human
>   semblance,
> and his form beyond that of mortals— . . .

He was despised and rejected by others;
    a man of suffering and acquainted with infirmity;
and as one from whom others hide their faces
    he was despised, and we held him of no account . . .

But he was wounded for our transgressions,
    crushed for our iniquities;
upon him was the punishment that made us whole,
    and by his bruises we are healed . . .

The righteous one, my servant, shall make many
            righteous,
    and he shall bear their iniquities.
Therefore I will allot him a portion with the great,
    and he shall divide the spoil with the strong;
because he poured out himself to death,
    and was numbered with the transgressors;
yet he bore the sin of many,
    and made intercession for transgressors.
        (Is 52:13–14; 53:3, 5, 11–12)

Jesus and the Suffering Servant

It does not need a great stretch of the imagination to see why this song
of the suffering servant is seen as a foretelling of the passion of Jesus Christ.
As matter of fact, it is chanted in the liturgy of Good Friday. It needs, however, to be interpreted. A prevalent view among people of all cultures and
religions takes suffering as a punishment of sin. The Hindus would attribute
it to present or past misdeeds, reaching back to a previous birth, if necessary. In the Bible, Job's friends try to convince him that his illness and mis-
fortune are the result of his sins (Jb 4). When they meet a man born blind,
the disciples of Jesus ask him, "Rabbi, who sinned, this man or his parents,
that he was born blind?" (Jn 9:3). Since both the suffering servant and Jesus
Christ are seen as innocent, it is then understood that they are "paying" for
the sins of others. This world view can be seen in the song of the suffering
servant as well as in the many interpretations of the passion of Jesus Christ.

Today we do not feel comfortable with a punishing God. Jesus revealed
to us a loving and forgiving God, the model being the father of the prodigal son. We can therefore set aside this interpretation of the suffering of the
innocent as punishment for sin. The innocent person, however, does suffer.
Jesus suffers even unto death. This suffering is imposed by the "wicked." In

the case of Jesus, his defense of the poor and the marginalized and his criticism of empty ritual enrage the Jewish leaders, who seek to do away with him. But the attitude of the innocent to such imposed suffering is not passive but active. They make it an occasion for self-gift, which is total when it involves death. It becomes self-emptying, self-surrender. It is an antidote to the pride and self-sufficiency of the wicked. By their self-gift they draw others too—even their enemies—into the process. The others, then, participating in the self-emptying of the innocent, participate in the fullness of life that God gives them. This is how the self-giving death of the innocent becomes fruitful. They die not only for themselves but also for the others, that is, in solidarity with them. All those who share their death will also share their life. In this way they are servants of God and of the others. An example would be soldiers fighting for their country. They are ready to go on a mission that is sure to bring death. Death itself is inflicted on them by the enemy. But the soldiers embrace that death in defense of their country, out of love for their countrymen. Though they die, their country is saved by their bold gesture. Soldiers and country are in solidarity with each other. The soldiers are servants of their country and their people.

The suffering servant does not choose suffering but is ready to face it when it is imposed. Suffering then becomes life giving, not as punishment, but as an expression of love and self-gift. It does not yield merit, as it is sometimes understood. Life is not merited by suffering and death. Life is always a gift of God. God does not reward suffering but responds generously with new life to a self-gift of life in death, though this death itself is imposed by someone else. This self-gift can take other forms, like living for others, serving, and caring.

The image of Jesus as servant is therefore a rich symbol that resonates at the moral, spiritual, and even metaphysical levels. To serve others is to be humble. To be humble is eventually to empty oneself in total self-gift, which attracts God's gift of new and abundant life. To empty oneself totally may mean death. Death becomes the source of new life. Here we come to the metaphysical level. Dying is part of the necessary process of life. But it need not be undergone passively; it can be assumed and lived consciously and actively. This spiritual metaphysics can be further explored in dialogue with Asian religious traditions.

Self-emptying and Egolessness

The reason why the Buddhist monk from Sri Lanka chose to represent Christ washing the feet of his disciples is probably the egolessness that Jesus shows in this gesture. Jesus is emptying himself to be at the service of the others. Achieving egolessness is the goal of Buddhist *sadhana* or religious practice. Meditating on his experience of suffering, the Buddha intuits that desire or clinging is the reason for suffering. At the root of clinging is the ego that clings to various objects of its desire. Buddha suggests that the ego itself and the objects it clings to are all impermanent, changing, without fixed substance. Modern Buddhists like Bhikku Buddhadasa of Thailand and Thich Nhat Hanh of Vietnam suggest that the reality that is moving and changing is not "nothing" but interdependent. No element of reality is absolute and self-sufficient in itself. Everything is dependent on everything else. Reality is like a net that has many knots. A knot has no meaning in itself. Each knot is dependent on the other knots in constituting the net. If I pull one knot, all other knots are immediately affected. For any single knot to think of itself as absolute and attempt to subordinate and use other knots to its own purpose destroys the net. It is in being dependent that a knot achieves its purpose. Egotism is a knot seeking to stand alone, making itself the center of reality. Egolessness is when a knot realizes its dependence, accepts it, and collaborates with all the other knots. Egolessness is an experience of self-emptying and solidarity. Jesus washing the feet of his disciples is seen as an egoless person. He is a man for others. He finds the meaning of life in serving others, not in being served. We may not accept the Buddhist metaphysical construction of reality, but the ideal of egolessness, of self-emptying and self-surrender, of loving and serving others, of giving oneself even unto death are part of the practice and teaching of Jesus. To call Jesus servant is to affirm that he is egoless and self-emptying. Freeing oneself of one's clingings, including the clinging to one's own self, can be part of Christian *sadhana*. Washing of one another's feet can be its ideal experience and expression.

Self-emptying and *Advaita*

The Indian perspective of *advaita* or non-duality can also throw light on the self-emptying. *Advaita* affirms that reality is one, not two. There is one absolute Reality. The other realities are dependent on it. They are not totally different from it or opposed to it. Various schools differ about how "real" the other realities are. But whatever their level of reality, they are dependent on the one Absolute. Problems start when a relative reality thinks of itself as absolute and tries to make itself the center of the universe, demanding that everything else should be at its service. As such a demand does not correspond to Reality, it is bound to lead to disorder and suffering. Liberation from such disorder and suffering comes when the relatively or dependent real becomes aware of its dependence, accepts it, and lives it. The goal of advaitic sadhana is to achieve this realization. This involves emptying one-self of one's self-sufficiency and acknowledging one's total dependence on the Absolute. At a spiritual level this means total selflessness so that the self loses itself in the Absolute and the Absolute lives and acts in the self. To realize such oneness with the Absolute is also to become aware that all realities or beings are one with the Absolute. Therefore, one is related to everything else in and through the Absolute. One then sees the Absolute in everything and everything in the Absolute. The Isa Upanishad says:

> Behold the universe in the glory of God;
>   and all that lives and moves on earth.
> Leaving the transient, find joy in the Eternal.
>
> Who sees all beings in the Self
> and the Self in all beings
> loses all fear.

Mahatma Gandhi used these words to summarize his own spirituality. To empty oneself and be one with the Absolute can then mean that one is at the disposal of the others in whom one perceives the Absolute. When one empties oneself, one is filled with the Absolute and in and through it with everything. All conflicts born of egotism disappear. Peace and harmony reign. Such an ideal of seeing the Absolute in everything and everything in the Absolute is very similar to the effort of finding God in all things and all things in God suggested by Ignatius of Loyola.

Not speaking about God, the Buddhists speak only of emptiness. Contemplating the Absolute, the Hindus speak of the fullness from which we all receive, empty as we are. The fullness empties itself in us. The Mundaka Upanishad gives us a vision of this fullness, the word Brahman denoting the Absolute.

> In the supreme golden chamber is Brahman indivisible and pure. He is the radiant light of all lights, and this knows he who knows Brahman. There the sun shines not, nor the moon, nor the stars; lightnings shine not there and much less earthly fire. From his light all these give light; and his radiance illumines all creation.

Emptiness becomes fullness, and fullness empties itself. They are two poles of a dialectic, like the yin and the yang of the Chinese tradition. In personal terms it will be a mystery of ongoing, mutual, total self-gift. The mysterious process starts with God.

Christian Self-emptying

Jesus, of course, is neither Buddhist nor Hindu. Hinduism, Buddhism, and Christianity may differ in their metaphysical elaborations. But at the level of *sadhana* they seem to converge. The goal of life is to become selfless and to be at the service of the others. Jesus is a model of this *sadhana*. He speaks of selfless love and service of and sharing with others. After telling his disciples to "love one another as I have loved you," he goes on to add, "No one has greater love than this, to lay down one's life for one's friends" (Jn 15:12–13). Coming a day before his own death, it spells out the deeper meaning of that death.

We saw earlier how Paul sees Christ Jesus, being in the form of God, emptying himself to become a human servant (Phil 2:6–8). Here we have God's self-emptying to become human. Christians who are metaphysically minded can push this reflection further to see self-emptying as a characteristic of God. We believe that God is Father, Son, and Holy Spirit. Their communion in one God can be seen as a constant act of mutual self-giving. The Father empties himself in the Son and the Spirit. Today, it is through the Son and the Spirit that we encounter the Father. We do not experience the Father somehow in himself. The Son empties himself in the Father and in the Spirit. The Son goes away to send the Spirit: "It is to your advantage that I go away, for if I do not go away, the Advocate will not come to you; but if I go, I will send him to you" (Jn 16:7). The Son also empties himself in the Father. Jesus says, "The Son can do nothing on his own, but what he sees the Father doing" (Jn 5:19). Paul says, "When all things are subjected to him, then the Son himself will also be subjected to the one who put all things in subjection under him, so that God may be all in all" (1 Cor 15:28). The self-emptying of the Son is preceded by the self-emptying of all things in the Son. The Spirit self-empties in the Father and the Son. Jesus says, "When the Spirit of truth comes, he will guide you into all the truth; for he will not speak on his own, but will speak whatever he hears" (Jn 16:13). Therefore the Trinity is a communion of mutual self-emptying. Jesus as the servant is not only a model for our self-emptying service to one another but also a symbol of trinitarian self-emptying. Jesus also speaks of this mutual self-emptying as mutual indwelling and associates all of us with it when he prays "as you, Father, are in me and I am in you, may they also be in us" (Jn 17:21).

Jesus as Servant

Being a servant in the manner of Jesus can lead us to *advaitic* and trinitarian mysticism. But let us not forget that it all starts with being a servant.

We started this chapter by contemplating Jesus washing the feet of his disciples. This example of Jesus strikes us only because we associate such an action with servants. But service takes various forms all through the life of Jesus. Soon after his baptism Jesus is tempted to use his God-given powers for his own convenience and glorification. Jesus resists the temptation and resolves to use his power only to help the people. He will not work a miracle to feed himself (Mt 4:3–4). But he will feed five thousand and more people in the desert (Mt 14:13–21). He heals all those who seek his help. He goes out of his way to dialogue with people like the Samaritan and Canaanite women. He defends the sinful woman who washes his feet with her tears and wipes them with her hair. He protects the woman who is taken in adultery. He visits the houses of Zacchaeus and Matthew, though they were known to be tax collectors and despised by others. He does not wait for people to come to him. He goes where they are, to the beaches, to the synagogues, to the marketplace, to the Temple. He chooses a band of simple fishermen and trains them to become his apostles. He tells simple stories and parables to make his points. He does not hesitate to leave home and family and to live on the hospitality of the people. He does not pretend to be either a political leader or a great scholar of the scriptures. He is at the service of the people. He challenges them but never dominates them.

Christians as Servants

Christians are called to be a community of servants, loving and serving one another. But the Christian community today is structured on the pattern of the political groups of the ancient Romans. Hierarchy and power seem more important to this community than service. Even when we speak about communion, it is qualified as hierarchical communion. A lot of effort is made to preserve the distinctions between priests and people, men and women. Special dresses, titles, and ceremonies set the people in power apart from the others. Obedience rather than service is seen as the principle of unity in the community. Hierarchical domination is claimed in the name of God. So it is unquestionable, absolute. It is basically a political order in which one speaks of power, jurisdiction, obedience, and sanctions. The pope, for some centuries, claimed absolute power, both sacred and secular, over the world. A community focused on service will depend more on dialogue, discussion, consultation, collaboration, and coordination than on authority and obedience. Discernment will come out of mutual listening to the Spirit of God, who is present and active in everyone. Collegiality will not only be a formal framework but a real sharing of responsibility. All people will be equal before God. Equality of status, however, does not exclude differentiation of roles and

responsibilities. But these are not titles for superiority of status or for domi-
nating power.

Christians are also called to be servants in the world. Unfortunately, till
the Second Vatican Council, Christians tried to dominate the world in the
sphere of religion. We claimed to have the only true religion. We looked
down on everyone else as imperfect and inadequate. Some of us still do so.
Today we recognize in other religions some good and holy elements. We try
to cultivate an atmosphere of dialogue with the world, with cultures and religions, and with other churches and ecclesial communities. Even then, I do
not think that we will be ready to consider ourselves the servants of the others. I think that an attitude of service will be easier for us if our focus is not
on ourselves but on God and God's kingdom. It is customary to speak of the
church as the sacrament of the kingdom of God. The term *sacrament* is
explained as "sign and instrument." Since the kingdom of God and the
church are human and social realities, it would be better to speak today of
the church as symbol and servant. The church then is the symbol and servant of the kingdom of God. Its identity is that of a servant. The nature of
this service will be clear if we realize that the Spirit of God continues to be
active in the world, in people, and in cultures and religions. Our desire to
serve urges us to dialogue with all people of good will. The reason for dialogue is our respect both for the freedom and dignity of all human beings,
whatever their caste, color, race, or religion, and for the freedom of the Spirit
of God, who is present and active in them. The character of our dialogue
will be very different, depending on whether we put ourselves in the driver's
seat of history or we let the Spirit of God be the driver. The key to an attitude of service is the realization that we are nothing and that God is everything in us. Instead, we tend to feel self-important as representatives of God
inheriting God's authority and power.

Conclusion

Humility and an attitude of service are not merely moral qualities. They
are not a strategy or a manner of behavior. Humility is truth. Jesus had to
empty himself in becoming human. On the contrary we *are* empty. We are
nothing. But with the gifts of God that we have received we pretend to be
important and powerful. A feeling of emptiness does not come naturally to
us. That is why the goal of *sadhana* is to become aware of what we really
are. Becoming aware of our total dependence on God, we also realize our
links to and dependence on everyone and everything. Mutual service then
becomes our way of being in the world. An Indo-Pakistan Muslim leader of
the last century, Mawlana Sayyid Abul A'la Mawdudi (1903–79), used to

speak of *theo-democracy*. God is the only Lord. All of us are God's crea-
tures. We are equals before God. The appropriate political order for a group
of equals is democracy. But since all of us are seeking to do God's will, it
will be a democracy that will be subject to God—a *theo-democracy*. Anyone in authority in such a group is only playing a role and is answerable both
to God and to the people. Contemporary democracy is defined as govern-
ment of the people, by the people, for the people. It depends on the balancing of individual self-interests. It is secular in the sense of being without
God. The community is ruled by the majority for convenience. Competition
leads to economic, political, and social inequality, though a framework of
formal political equality, expressed in the vote, is maintained. A conflict of
interests is built into such a structure. In such a context, the ideal of *theo-
democracy* is worth thinking about, provided God is the God of all, not
merely of one particular religion. Given the kind of social conflicts we have
around the world today, *theo-democracy* may be an ideal. But it is an ideal
that is worth pursuing. Perhaps the church and the religious congregations
can start practicing it as models for political groups to follow. That would be
the reality of authentic communion.

9

Jesus,
the Compassionate

When we read through the life of Jesus in the gospels, an image that comes to us strongly is that of the compassionate Jesus. People, especially the poor, the suffering, and the marginalized, crowd around him. He heals their illnesses, drives away the evil spirits that afflict them, frees them from the burden of their sins, and gives them their dignity as humans and the children of God. He is the healer, the reconciler, the savior. He suffers with those who suffer in order to liberate them from their suffering. Indeed, the word *compassionate* means "to suffer with."

In Asia the term *compassionate* evokes the figure of the Buddha. The Buddha achieves liberation from suffering through contemplation on the impermanent nature of all things. Once liberated, he is not satisfied with enjoying the state of freedom and peace. He looks around him at those who are still suffering and struggling in the world. He communicates to them the good news of his own liberation and guides them toward their own liberation. Compassion—*maitri, karuna*—is one of the main Buddhist virtues. In the Buddhist tradition the bodhisattva is the model of a compassionate person. Having achieved personal liberation, the bodhisattva delays the personal enjoyment of it in order to help everyone become liberated, realizing that there is no full liberation till everyone and everything are liberated, since the whole of reality is interconnected. We have seen above, in Chapter 2, that the Buddhists in Asia consider Jesus a bodhisattva.

By calling Jesus compassionate, I have no intention of comparing him to the Buddha or of making him a bodhisattva. I am not saying that Jesus is a bodhisattva or Buddha. Compassionate is an image that has a resonance in Asia because of the Buddhist tradition. Asians who hear the story of Jesus will perceive him as a compassionate person. How he is compassionate, however, has to be discovered, not by comparing him to the Buddha, but by looking at his own compassionate words and deeds. The term *compassion* acquires a specific connotation when we think of Jesus. He is compassionate like no other. In the following pages we look at the many ways in which Jesus manifests his compassion toward the people. We discover that his compassion takes on a special meaning when he dies and rises again to new life. The Buddha did not want to talk about God or about life after death. He did not deny them, but he left them unsaid. The compassion of Jesus operates around God's gift of abundant life, which he not only promises but shares with people. Sharing their suffering he empowers them to respond to God's gift of life in a creative way.

A Man of Compassion

We are told many times in the gospels that crowds of people gather around Jesus. Matthew summarizes the ministry of Jesus at the beginning of his gospel:

> Jesus went throughout Galilee, teaching in their synagogues and pro-claiming the good news of the kingdom and curing every disease and every sickness among the people. So his fame spread throughout all Syria, and they brought to him all the sick, those who were afflicted with various diseases and pains, demoniacs, epileptics, and paralytics, and he cured them. And great crowds followed him. (Mt 4:23–25)

These crowds evoke the compassion of Jesus. In another story we see a dramatic expression of it. He had sent his disciples to proclaim the good news of the kingdom. They came back rejoicing in their success. Jesus took them aside to a desert place for some well-deserved rest. But the people find out where they are headed and go there before them. Mark narrates:

> As he went ashore, he saw a great crowd; and he had compassion for them, because they were like sheep without a shepherd; and he began to teach them many things. (Mk 6:34)

Jesus does not stop with teaching. Seeing that it is late he wants to make sure that the people get something to eat. He ends up miraculously feeding five thousand men, not counting women and children. Matthew actually points to the implication of this compassion in one of his summaries by quoting Isaiah:

> That evening they brought to him many who were possessed with demons; and he cast out the spirit with a word, and cured all who were sick. This was to fulfill what had been spoken through the prophet Isaiah, "He took our infirmities and bore our diseases." (Mt 8:16–17)

The reference is obviously to the passion of Jesus, which is presented as an act of compassion and solidarity.

What he does with the crowds of people corresponds to his own awareness of what God has called him to do. In the synagogue of Nazareth, where he grew up, he quotes approvingly the text of Isaiah, applying it to himself:

> "The Spirit of the Lord is upon me,
>> because he has anointed me to bring the good news
>>> to the poor.
>
> He has sent me to proclaim release to the captives
>> and recovery of sight to the blind,
>> to let the oppressed go free,
>> to proclaim the year of the Lord's favor." (Lk 4:18–19)

Jesus presents the same image of himself when John the Baptist sends his disciples to ask him, "Are you the one who is to come?" Luke reports, "Jesus had just then cured many people of diseases, plagues, and evil spirits, and had given sight to many who were blind." Then Jesus goes on to answer John's disciples, "Go and tell John what you have seen and heard: the blind receive their sight, the lame walk, the lepers are cleansed, the deaf hear, the dead are raised, the poor have good news brought to them" (Lk 7:18–23).

Jesus, the Healer

To a superficial observer of the life of Jesus, he would have appeared as a healer. He heals the sick, gives sight to the blind, makes the lame walk, cleanses the lepers, enables the mute to speak, even raises the dead to life. Every page of the gospels gives us examples of these healings, so detailed references to these stories are not necessary. What is important to understand are the many dimensions of these healings. First of all, they often seem psychosomatic in nature. Sickness is linked to possession by evil spirits. Matthew reports: "A demoniac was brought to him. And when the demon had been cast out, the one who had been mute spoke" (Mt 9:32–33). Another demoniac is cured of blindness. Similarly, Jesus cures an epileptic boy by casting out a demon from him (Mt 17:14–18).

Sickness is also linked to sinfulness and healing to forgiveness. The people bring a paralytic to Jesus. He tells the sick man: "Take heart, son; your sins are forgiven." He goes on to say, "Stand up, take your bed and go to your home." The sick man does so (Mt 9:2–8). Jesus heals a sick man who had been waiting for thirty-eight years to be healed near the pool Beth-zatha in Jerusalem. The Jews protest because he heals him on the sabbath day. When

Jesus meets him again, he tells him: "See, you have been made well. Do not sin any more, so that nothing worse happens to you" (Jn 5:14).

Sometimes healing may not be merely physical, but also psychological and spiritual. The forgiveness of sins brings a sense of freedom. Jesus is at the table in the house of a Pharisee (Lk 7:36–50). A sinful woman approaches him, weeping, bathes his feet with her tears, wipes them with her hair, kisses them, and anoints them with an ointment. Jesus compares her gesture with the poor welcome from the Pharisee, who did not provide water to wash his feet, kiss him, or offer oil for his head. Then he tells the woman: "Your sins are forgiven." He recognizes and appreciates her great love. That appreciation must have affirmed her dignity and self-esteem and freed her from the kind of oppressive attitudes of the people around her. They may not have changed their attitudes. But she is now free enough not to bother about their opinions. She feels empowered to go out to love and serve others.

On another occasion the Jews bring him a woman caught in adultery so that she can be stoned, according to their law. Jesus looks at her and at them. Then he tells them calmly, "Let anyone among you who is without sin be the first to throw a stone at her." The crowd melts away. Jesus tells the woman: "Go your way, and from now on do not sin again" (Jn 8:1–11). The woman must have felt freed, encouraged, and empowered to help other women victimized by society.

Healing can also be social. The Jews ostracize those whom they consider sinners like the tax collectors and prostitutes. Jesus, on the contrary, seems to seek out their company. He has compassion for them. He wants to heal their hurts and restore their human dignity. Matthew, the tax collector, is called by Jesus to become his disciple. He throws a party in his house. Jesus joins the party. The Pharisees object to the gesture. Jesus tells them: "Those who are well have no need of a physician, but those who are sick. Go and learn what this means, 'I desire mercy, not sacrifice.' For I have come to call not the righteous but sinners" (Mt 9:9–13). Even as he is showing his solidarity with the socially marginalized, Jesus uses the metaphor of healing. Such an expression of solidarity with them can lead to a real transformation. We see an example of this when Jesus visits the home of Zacchaeus, another tax collector. Zacchaeus has made an extra effort to see Jesus by climbing a tree. Still, the visit of Jesus to his house must have been a surprise. He has been recognized as a person with dignity and as a host. The impact seems immediate. Zacchaeus declares, "Look, half of my possessions, Lord, I will give to the poor; and if I have defrauded anyone of anything, I will pay back four times as much." It is significant that Jesus calls this change of mind salvation. He declares: "Today salvation has come to this house, because he too is a son of Abraham. For the Son of Man has come to seek out and save the lost" (Lk 19:1–10). Salvation then is transformation and empowerment to be more just and loving.

Another social dimension of healing is seen when the forgiveness and love that God offers us reach out to others through us. This is summarized in the prayer that Jesus taught his disciples: "And forgive us our debts, as we also have forgiven our debtors" (Mt 6:12). Jesus illustrates this in a parable, in which he speaks about a rich man who forgives the debts of his servants while one of his servants refuses to forgive his own debtors. Everyone sees the injustice of such an action. That servant is taken to task by the master (Mt 18:23–35). Jesus elaborates the principle of forgiveness and reconciliation when he says:

> "When you are offering your gift at the altar, if you remember that your brother or sister has something against you, leave your gift there before the altar and go; first be reconciled to your brother or sister, and then come and offer your gift." (Mt 5:23–24)

Jesus pushes the teaching further when he says:

> "Love your enemies and pray for those who persecute you, so that you may be children of your Father in heaven; for he makes his sun rise on the evil and on the good and sends the rain on the righteous and on the unrighteous . . . Be perfect, therefore, as your heavenly Father is perfect." (Mt 5:44–45, 48)

Luke has a different way of phrasing the last sentence: "Be merciful, just as your Father is merciful" (Lk 6:36). In Asia we can further rephrase it: "Be compassionate, just as your Father is compassionate." In the gospel of John, Jesus proposes himself as a model of love. He tells the disciples, "Love one another as I have loved you" (Jn 15:12). He illustrates further what this love involves. "No one has greater love than this, to lay down one's life for one's friends" (Jn 15:13). Finally, he suggests the communion between him and his Father as the model of communion among ourselves and with God: "that they may all be one. As you, Father, are in me and I am in you, may they also be in us" (Jn 17:21). Such a communion in love is the perfection of salvation.

Looking at these different events of healing we see an image of salvation emerging. People are freed from various sorts of oppression—physical, psychological, social, and spiritual. They are recognized and affirmed as persons. They are reconciled to one another and to God. Love and justice characterize their lives afterward. There is a communion of love and life of which God becomes the center. This is salvation.

Healing and Faith

Looking at the various events of healing in the life of Jesus we find a close link between healing and faith. Jesus heals a centurion's servant just by a word of command. But he attributes the healing to the faith of the centurion, who suggests that Jesus need not take the trouble of coming all the way to his house because a word of command would do. Jesus then says, "Go; let it be done for you according to your faith" (Mt 8:5–13).

At another time, he is pressed by a crowd as he is going to the house of Jairus, whose daughter lay dying. In the crowd is a woman who hopes to be cured of her hemorrhages by touching his cloak. She does so and is cured. But it does not go unnoticed by Jesus, who feels power go from him. He looks at her with compassion and tells her, "Take heart, daughter; your faith has made you well" (Mt 9:20–22).

He heals two blind men who tell him that he can cure them of their blindness if he wishes. He heals them by touching their eyes and telling them, "According to your faith, let it be done to you" (Mt 9:27–29).

A Canaanite woman asks him to free her daughter from a demon. Jesus hesitates and says that he is sent only to work among the Jews and puts her off by saying, "It is not fair to take the children's food and throw it to the dogs." She challenges him, "Yes, Lord, yet even the dogs eat the crumbs that fall from their masters' table." Jesus then yields and answers her: "Woman, great is your faith! Let it be done for you as you wish" (Mt 15:21–28).

When the disciples are unable to heal an epileptic boy with a demon, he blames them for their lack of faith. He then goes on to sing the merits of true faith: "If you have faith the size of a mustard seed, you will say to this mountain, 'Move from here to there,' and it will move; and nothing will be impossible for you" (Mt 17:20–21).

Before raising Lazarus, the brother of Martha and Mary, he demands an affirmation of faith from Martha: "I am the resurrection and the life. Those who believe in me, even though they die, will live, and everyone who lives and believes in me will never die. Do you believe this?" Martha confesses, "Yes, Lord, I believe that you are the Messiah, the some of God, the one coming into the world" (Jn 11:25–27). Then Jesus raises Lazarus from the dead.

The best example of faith is Mary, the mother of Jesus. There is no more wine at the wedding feast at Cana. Mary requests that Jesus do something. Jesus seems hesitant, saying, "My hour has not yet come." But Mary's faith does not waver. She tells the servants, "Do whatever he tells you." The servants fill the jars with water, as ordered by Jesus, and the water turns into wine (Jn 2:1–10).

In all these cases faith seems to provoke miracles. Jesus attributes the healing not to his power but to their faith.

On the contrary, where there is no faith, there is no healing. Jesus goes to Nazareth, "and he did not do many deeds of power there, because of their unbelief" (Mt 13:58). Seeing Jesus coming to their boat by walking on the water, Peter asks him to let him (Peter) come to him (Jesus) on the water. Jesus says yes, and Peter jumps into the water. But then, threatened by the waves, he is afraid and starts sinking. Jesus reprimands him, "You of little faith, why did you doubt?" (Mt 14:31). Similarly, when the disciples ask Jesus why they could not cast out the demon from an epileptic boy brought to them, Jesus answers frankly, "Because of your little faith" (Mt 17:20). In all these instances of healing or of its lack we see a dialectic between the power of Jesus to heal and the power of the faith of the people who receive healing. The power and the readiness of Jesus to heal seem to be always there. That power is unleashed, so to speak, by the faith of those who are asking for or are engaged in healing. Without faith the healing will not take place.

Healing and Salvation

Jesus does not set about healing every sick or possessed person in Palestine. His healing miracles are only symbols of his mission of salvation. They make symbolically present God's saving action in Jesus, which is seen as a freeing action making people whole in every sense. Salvation itself is seen as life. Meditating on the Word, John says, "In the beginning was the Word, and the Word was with God and the Word was God. He was in the beginning with God. All things came into being through him, and without him not one thing came into being. What has come into being in him was life, and the life was the light of all people" (Jn 1:1–4). This Word, which is at the origin of all life, becomes flesh in Jesus. John then goes on to say, "From his fullness we have all received, grace upon grace" (Jn 1:16). God's gift to the world in Jesus is life. Jesus himself tells Nicodemus, "God so loved the world that he gave his only Son, so that everyone who believes in him may not perish but may have eternal life" (Jn 3:17). Jesus indicates through his teaching that this fullness of life that God gives us is the sharing of life in a community through mutual forgiveness, love, and service. To live in such communion is salvation. This can happen already in this life, and it will continue for ever.

God's gift of life is unconditioned. It is always there for us. The symbol of this is the father in the story of the prodigal son. The father is waiting for the wayward son to come back, ready to forgive him everything unconditionally (Lk 15:11–24). The son, of course, has to come back, but he does not deserve his father's pardon and reintegration into the family. God's gift is not

in any way merited by our good deeds. But at the same time God has created us in God's image as free persons. We have to accept God's gift. We
have to say yes. In doing so we recognize our own helplessness and our total
dependence on God. Our inability to be open and empty in this way so as
to be filled by God is the problem. The fault that Jesus finds with the Pharisees is precisely this. They are so self-sufficient. They think that they can
merit God's life by their faithful observance of the law: the prescriptions with
regard to the sabbath, the rules of purity and pollution, the schedule of
prayers and fasts. Jesus keeps telling them that what is required is not their
own effort at acquiring life but humility and selflessness that accepts God's
gift. He tells his disciples: "Unless you change and become little children, you
will not enter the kingdom of heaven. Whoever becomes humble like this
child is the greatest in the kingdom of heaven" (Mt 18:3–4). We get the same
message when Jesus prays to the Father, "I thank you, Father, Lord of
heaven and earth, because you have hidden these things from the wise and
the intelligent and have revealed them to infants; yes, Father, such was your
gracious will" (Mt 11:25–26). Once again, Mary gives us an example of such
openness and dependence. When the angel Gabriel is talking to her, she
opens herself up, "Here am I, the servant of the Lord; let it be with me according to your word" (Lk 1:38). The Holy Spirit then overshadows her and
Jesus is conceived in her womb. Mary does nothing but say yes. In her song
of praise and thanksgiving—the Magnificat—we hear:

> "My soul magnifies the Lord,
>   and my spirit rejoices in God my savior,
> for he has looked with favor on the lowliness of his
>   servant . . .
> He has brought down the powerful from their thrones,
>   and lifted up the lowly;
> he had filled the hungry with good things,
>   and sent the rich away empty." (Lk 1:47–48, 52–53)

Jesus also illustrates this attitude with a parable.

> "Two men went up to the temple to pray, one a Pharisee and the other
> a tax-collector. The Pharisee, standing by himself, was praying thus,
> 'God, I thank you that I am not like other people: thieves, rogues,
> adulterers, or even like this tax-collector. I fast twice a week; I give a
> tenth of all my income.' But the tax-collector, standing far off, would
> not even look up to heaven, but was beating his breast and saying,
> 'God, be merciful to me a sinner!' I tell you, this man went down to
> his home justified rather than the other; for all who exalt themselves

will be humbled, but all who humble themselves will be exalted." (Lk 18:10–14)

This is not a moral lesson on humility. This is about the requirements necessary for justification or salvation. The Pharisee sought to save himself with his good behavior—fasting and almsgiving—and he did not succeed. The tax collector confesses his helplessness but pleads for God's mercy—and he is saved.

The obstacles to salvation, therefore, are not the many sins that we may commit due to our weakness, of which we later repent. The real block is egotism, self-sufficiency, and pride. When we actively seek to conquer salvation, we miss it. When we humbly accept salvation as a gift from God, we receive it in abundance. This is the meaning behind this paradox: "Those who want to save their lives will lose it, and those who lose their life for my sake will find it" (Mt 16:25). The measure of the abundance of God's gift of life is not our merits but God's generosity. The crucial element in the process of salvation is our openness to accept it as a gift of God, since God's gift is always there. Being sure of God's unbounded love, we are ready to abandon ourselves to God. God then saves us. This egoless abandonment is the faith that Jesus expects when he heals someone. The gospel speaks of poverty, humility, faith. In Asia we would rather speak of egolessness, surrender, action without attachment. It is not giving up things but abandoning one's self. But giving up things may be a sign of our desire to give up ourselves. This faith or egolessness refrains from every kind of immoral and unjust behavior. It finds positive expression in the love of the other. In loving the other we are ready to give up everything. We do not hold on to anything as our own. We are willing to give until it hurts, until death. "No one has greater love than this, to lay down one's life for one's friends" (Jn 15:13). Death becomes the way to life, because God responds to our surrender with the gift of life. This is also the message of the resurrection of Jesus.

Jesus, the Savior

Jesus saves us precisely by enabling us to respond to God in humility and faith, in egolessness and surrender, and thus to receive God's gift of life. He enables us by being in solidarity with us. Our egotism finds expression in various sorts of internal blocks and external malfunctionings or diseases. These lead to suffering. Being in solidarity with us, Jesus is compassionate. That is to say, he suffers with us. He makes suffering a manifestation of egolessness. Jesus is born into a world full of suffering. He does not go looking for suffering. He seeks, rather, to free people from suffering. But then suffering is imposed on him by others. Jesus joins the ranks of the victims.

However, by accepting the suffering as a manifestation of love and self-gift he shows that suffering does not have the last word, that suffering can be overcome, that life endures in spite of suffering. He cannot abolish suffering from the world, because he cannot, on his own, do away with egotistical people in the world. But he can show how suffering can be made into a force for transformation. That is what he does. He makes us realize that our suffering is not punishment for our sins. By accepting suffering we can transform it as a symbol of our self-gift.

By becoming compassionate with us, Jesus enables us to become compassionate with him. He shares our suffering, and in that very process we share his suffering. Overcoming suffering in himself, he helps us also to overcome suffering in ourselves. We cannot do away with suffering in this life. But God's gift of life transcends suffering. We can live this life even in the midst of suffering. Suffering does not touch us in our depths. It is seen and experienced as something transient. When we reach this awareness and live the life given to us by God we are saved. This is how Jesus saves us. We share in salvation, which is a participation in the life of God, by becoming compassionate with him. Jesus the compassionate becomes Jesus the savior. Just as we share in his sufferings we also share in his resurrection, in his new life: "For if we have been united with him in a death like his, we will certainly be united with him in a resurrection like his" (Rom 6:5). This is the process of salvation.

We can try to understand further how Jesus actually saves us by analyzing the various dimensions of salvation. He saves us by freeing us, by forgiving us, by loving us, and by empowering or enabling us. Let us look these dimensions briefly.

We are born into a sinful world. We too become sinful by our own selfish actions. This sinfulness cripples us, making us sick, deaf-mutes, paralytics, and so on—to use the symbols that we see in the gospels. We are burdened spiritually, psychologically, and even physically. Jesus frees us from these burdens in two ways. He communicates to us God's forgiving love, provided we repent. He also frees us from our self-made structures of oppression. The law is one such oppressive structure, standing for all human-made structures. Paul shows us in his letters to the Romans and the Galatians how Jesus frees us from the oppressions of the law. He gives us the Holy Spirit, who is the source of our inner freedom, making us children of God:

All who are led by the Spirit of God are children of God. For you did not receive a spirit of slavery to fall back into fear, but you have received a spirit of adoption. When we cry, "Abba! Father!" it is that very Spirit bearing witness with our spirit that we are children of God, and if children, then heirs, heirs of God and joint heirs with Christ. (Rom 8:14–17)

The perfect example of this in the gospel is the sinful woman who comes to Jesus when he is at table with a Pharisee. We have seen this story earlier. She washes his feet with her tears, wipes them with her hair, kisses them, and anoints them with ointment. Everyone who knows that the woman is a sinner is shocked to see Jesus, reputed to be a prophet, allow a sinful woman to touch him in this way. It is polluting, according to their law. Jesus simply asserts that the woman is no longer sinful. "Her sins, which were many, have been forgiven; hence she has shown great love" (Lk 7:47). There must have been an earlier encounter between the woman and Jesus, perhaps a silent one, during one of the journeys of Jesus. The woman has been touched by Jesus and repents of her misdeeds. She responds to his call to conversion. That repentance is enough for God to forgive her sins and make her whole. The woman responds to God's boundless forgiving love by an outpouring of love in her turn, of which Jesus becomes the object. Let us note that in the statement of Jesus, forgiveness precedes love: her sins have been forgiven, *hence* she has shown great love. The sinful woman is saved. She has become a child of God who can call God Abba! Father! Jesus has been compassionate to her. Freedom and forgiveness, love and life are intertwined in this divine-human dialogue.

This experience of salvation will not save her from continuing domination by the oppressive structures of her time and the consequent suffering. But the suffering will now acquire a new meaning. She will take it as a means of expressing her love, commitment, and loyalty. It will seem endurable and as nothing compared to the life—the freedom, joy, and peace—that she is now enjoying. This has been the experience of martyrs. Has not Jesus said, "Blessed are those who are persecuted for righteousness' sake, for theirs is the kingdom of heaven" (Mt 5:10)?

God's love and life not only frees us, but it also empowers and enables us. As Paul tells us, "The Spirit helps us in our weakness; for we do not know how to pray as we ought, but that very Spirit intercedes with sighs too deep for words" (Rom 8:26). Zacchaeus offers us an example of this empowerment. Being of short stature and anxious to see Jesus, he climbs a tree. Jesus visits his house. Zacchaeus tells Jesus, "Look, half of my possessions, Lord, I will give to the poor; and if I have defrauded anyone of anything, I will pay back four times as much." Jesus declares, "Today salvation has come to this house" (Lk 19:8–9). Zacchaeus has been transformed and has experienced salvation. The solidarity of Jesus with him is also a source of empowerment. This empowerment should be thought of not in material terms but in human terms. Jesus empowers us by his example and advice, by his compassion and love, by solidarity.

Conclusion

The compassionate Jesus heals and saves. He frees and makes whole. He energizes and empowers. He does so not in some material, automatic way but in a personal way, by loving us, by being a model, by enabling us from within, by being in solidarity with us. He shares with us *our* suffering and *his* resurrection. This experience of saving compassion and solidarity makes us realize that Jesus is not just another human being. In him God is present to us. What is necessary for us is not understanding the process or the metaphysics of this relationship. It is in any case beyond our understanding. It is a mystery. We can only experience it. We experience it precisely by being compassionate with Jesus, as he is compassionate with us, by dying with him so that we may rise with him. Jesus says, "Unless a grain of wheat falls into the earth and dies, it remains just a single grain; but if it dies, it bears much fruit" (Jn 12:24). In order to be fruitful, our ego must die. But dying is not enough. We must also abide in Jesus, because he also says, "Those who abide in me and I in them bear much fruit, because apart from me you can do nothing" (Jn 15:5). The compassion of Jesus leads us into deeper mystery, namely, divine communion: "As you, Father are in me and I am in you, may they also be in us" (Jn 17:21). These mysteries are not to be explained but lived.

The compassionate face of Jesus shows the feminine dimension of his personality. Jesus is the Word become human, not merely male. His male body does not limit his humanity, which includes male and female dimensions. Compassion is attributed to women, at least culturally. That is why some saints and poets in Christian tradition have seen God as mother. When God is seen primarily as male, people seek to complement God with a female figure like Mary in the Christian tradition, the various *devis* or goddesses in the Hindu tradition, and the KwanYin in the Chinese/Buddhist tradition. Christians also tend to see the Spirit of God as feminine. But I think that it is more proper to see a feminine dimension in God and in Jesus. In the compassion of Jesus it is the feminine aspect that dominates. Looking on Jesus as king and judge may highlight the male dimension. Jesus as savior points to the feminine aspect of caring, loving, serving, and self-giving.

The image of the compassionate Jesus also highlights aspects of solidarity in the process of salvation. To the gift of God corresponds our faith. Compassion, like freedom in dialogue, is a two-way process. It humanizes the salvific relationship, unlike salvific paradigms that are based on metaphors of redemption or punishment. Jesus the compassionate is indeed *Emmanuel*— God with us.

10

Jesus,
the Dancer

Music and especially dance are important experiences in life. When humans came together as a group, dance was probably their first means of collective self-expression. Looking at primal peoples today, we can say that it could have been a rain dance to make rain happen, or a hunting dance "magically" imitating the hunting process to assure success in hunting, or a triumphal dance to celebrate a victory in conflict, or a sacred dance to manifest basic attitudes of petition or thanksgiving before the Divine, or a harvest dance thanking God for a good harvest, or simply a celebration of life—of birth, marriage, or even death. There was a dance for every occasion. Music and even language as poetry must have had their origin in dance before they developed on their own. In language, of course, poetry precedes prose, and poetry must have been chanted. Dance involves the whole person, body and spirit, and the community. In the beginning people always danced as a community. Dancing together in rhythm to accompanying drums and other instruments is in itself an experience of and an exercise in community. The group shares not only common movements but shared meanings and emotions. The dance therefore builds up community. The whole person is involved in dancing. The chant as word engages the intellect and provides meaning. The music channels the various emotions according to the circumstances and sets the mood. The rhythm involves the body in movement. Since the dance involves the whole body, it can lead to integration and ecstasy. The followers of Caitanya in India and the Muslim dervishes of the Sufi tradition in the Middle East have explored this route to ecstasy. In primal religions dancing to a strong rhythm leads people to altered states of consciousness, experienced by them as possession by spirits or gods. A similar integration of the whole person in music and rhythm is also found in Zen practice in Japan. The classical dances of India, like Bharatanatyam, had their origin as dances in the temples or during sacred processions.

Experiencing integration and wholeness in dance, people imagine the whole cosmos as dancing. The movements of the stars and the planets are in rhythmic and dynamic tension. The harmonious movement of the *yin* and the *yang* in the Chinese and East Asian traditions is symbolic of the dance of the cosmos. The complementarity of the two principles lends rhythm and dynamism to ongoing movement. It may seem cyclic to a superficial observer. It is actually a spiral, indicating an evolution. We can see these dancing movements in the drifting clouds, the dancing streams, and the waving bamboos in Chinese paintings. In the Indian tradition Shiva dances the whole cosmic process from creation to dissolution. He is called the lord of the dance—Nataraja. Krishna, the manifestation of the Divine in human form, not only plays the flute but dances with the *gopis* or cow-herds, who symbolize the devotees. The music of his flute is said to attract the whole of creation to follow him. On the part of the devotees, dancing is an accepted form of expressing devotion in India.

The Bible speaks of David dancing before the Ark of the Covenant: "David and all the house of Israel were dancing before the Lord with all their might, with songs and lyres and harps and tambourines and castanets and cymbals" (2 Sm 6:5). This could not have been an isolated instance. It must have been accepted ritual practice. When the psalms praise God with the playing of musical, especially rhythmic instruments (Ps 150), they must have accompanied dancing. The Song of Songs can be imagined as a dancing duet. The early church appreciated music; Augustine says that singing is equivalent to praying twice. But musical instruments and dancing were associated with the cults of other religions and forbidden in the church. The organ and other instruments were introduced later. The domination of the monasteries in the evolution of the liturgy may have been responsible, not only for the avoidance of dance in worship, but also for not allowing music to develop beyond being a medium to chant the liturgical texts. Of course this did not hinder the Christian community from dancing at social celebrations. But dancing became stigmatized as a secular activity. Only after the Second Vatican Council have African and Asian dances entered the church and the liturgy. Elsewhere, too, dance has become part of the liturgy as a corporal expression of attitudes of adoration, thanksgiving, joy, and community. Young people are particularly open, sensitive, and responsive to such forms of self-expression in religion.

Even such openness to dancing in the liturgy may not prepare us to see God, especially Jesus, as a dancer. Our religious imagination sees the Father as a grave old man with long hair and a beard. Our favorite image of Jesus is of him hanging on the cross. The Spirit is the dove hovering between the Father and Jesus. Doves fly; they do not dance. However, I suggest that one of the images of Jesus in Asia could be the dancer, given the important role of dance, not merely as holistic means of self-expression, but also as a theo-logical perspective in Hinduism and Confucianism. We will understand this if we consider briefly the meaning of dance in human experience.

The Significance of Dance

Dance is an expression of joy and freedom. The image of a person with-out freedom is one who is tied down by something—care, force, fear, or responsibility. We speak of a free bird as one that is flying around. The near-est humans can come to flying is dancing, with body, arms, legs, head, and eyes engaged in free movement. Dancing is normally an expression of joy. We speak of someone dancing for joy. But one can express sorrow or pain in dance. One of the important sentiments conveyed by dance in India is the sorrow of separation from the lover. But the expression of joy is a more fre-quent theme.

Dance is purposeless action. Normally when we do something, we have a goal to achieve. We walk to a place. We work in the fields to make things grow. Sometimes we engage in activity that helps us to relax. Some people engage in gardening; others go for a walk; still others play a game. Action meets a need. But dancing has no purpose. We do not dance to impress others. When the whole community is dancing, there are no spectators. It is simply the sign of exuberance. It is self-expressive. In spirituality we speak about *nishkama karma* or desireless action. Every action is associated with a fruit or a goal or a purpose. We act because we desire the fruit. In doing so we become caught up in the cycle of *karma*. The way of escaping from the karmic cycle is to act without desire for the fruit. We do something be-cause it is our duty, our role in the cosmic happening. It is action without attachment. We are not obliged to do it. We do it spontaneously, freely. Acting without attachment or purpose is a state that we reach only with great effort and renunciation. Dancing is acting without attachment, without pur-pose, without the urge to achieve anything.

God has no needs. God creates the world and the humans spontaneously, freely, not to satisfy any need that God has. Rather, God is freely sharing God's life and joy with humans and the universe. God is dancing and invit-ing humans and the cosmos to dance along.

Dance is also like play. We do not play to achieve something. We do not run to go somewhere; rather, we run round and round on the field. We play for the fun of playing. We can enjoy the play even when we lose the game. A game is worth playing whether we win or lose. Playing in itself is worth-while and enjoyable. God's actions are often called *lila* or play in Indian tra-dition. It may seem meaningless or purposeless. It has no purpose outside itself. It is its own purpose. We can see parents playing with their children.

The creation of the cosmos is God's play. Creation exists because God continues to play. In the Hindu tradition, Shiva dances the cosmos into being. In the same spirit what we may experience as destruction and death are also God's play and dance. What we see as destruction is transformation in an ongoing dynamic movement from another point of view. Death leads to new life.

Dance is integral action. It integrates the whole body to enable it to move harmoniously. It integrates body and mind, intention and execution. When a Bharatanatyam dancer performs, her whole posture suggests and supports the gesture with the hands. Her head and eye movements also follow the gesture. That is how harmony of effect is achieved. Dance is the embodiment of dynamic movement. Ananda Coomaraswamy has said that the artistic genius of India is manifested in two outstanding images, one of peace and the other of pure movement. They are the seated Buddha lost in concentrated meditation symbolizing inner peace and tranquility and the dancing Nataraja, king of dancers, embodying cosmic movement in perfect equilibrium. Surprisingly, both lead to peace and harmony and to joy—inner in the Buddha and in integral human expression in Nataraja. It is the joy and peace of personal integration and fulfillment. But the dance of Nataraja is also cosmic.

Jesus, the Dancer

Thinking of Jesus as the dancer may surprise many. Jyoti Sahi, an Indian Christian artist, has painted and sculpted many images of the risen Christ dancing. In an unpublished manuscript he explains:

> To dance is to celebrate the body, to discover a new kind of freedom which is spirit filled. The spirits can chain the body, making of it a prison. But the spirit of life can liberate the body, and convert it into an instrument of joy. The healed person leaps for joy. This leap into the future is the essence of dance. To dance is to leap, to step over all the obstacles which hinder us on the way.

This is why resurrection can be imagined as dance. The risen Christ is dancing. Sara Grant, who had meditated long on the dynamic role of the Word and the Spirit in bringing the whole of creation together, says:

> The Word who became flesh and dwelt among us, who underwent death and is alive unto endless ages, can surely be called Lord of the Dance, who makes visible for us the hidden rhythms of the Creator Spirit at work within us and in our confused and torn-apart world to

bring all things to their mysterious consummation. In doing so he does not in any way diminish or destroy the marvelous variety of his creation, including the intuitions of the different cultural and religious traditions, but throws into brilliant relief all the treasures of inspiration and beauty they contain, his own truth and beauty in turn being enhanced in our eyes by their radiance.[1]

The term *Lord of the Dance* used by Sara Grant certainly refers to Nataraja—the dancing Shiva. But she reinterprets it as a name for Jesus, the Word incarnate. In both cases it has cosmic significance. For those who are not familiar with Indian tradition, it is good to note that the dancing Shiva is not a human manifestation or avatar of Shiva, as Rama and Krishna are avatars of Vishnu, but a symbolic image that expresses and manifests God's significance for us and for the cosmos.

Jyoti Sahi, on the other hand, links dance to healing and liberation. Let us explore the resonances that this image of Jesus evokes. While doing so, we have to keep in touch with a double dimension, personal and cosmic. Jesus is a person who dances in freedom, joy, a sense of fulfillment, and harmony. But Jesus also dances with and animates—is at the heart of—the cosmos, an image expressed in the following:

> I danced in the morning
> When the world was begun,
> And I danced in the moon
> And the stars and the sun,
> And I came down from heaven
> And I danced on the earth,
> At Bethlehem
> I had my birth.
>
> *Dance, then, wherever you may be,*
> *I am the Lord of the Dance, said he,*
> *And I'll lead you all, wherever you may be,*
> *And I'll lead you all in the Dance, said he*
>
> I danced for the scribe
> And the pharisee,
> But they would not dance
> And they wouldn't follow me.
> I danced for the fishermen,
> For James and John—
> They came with me
> And the Dance went on.

Chorus

I danced on the Sabbath
And I cured the lame;
The holy people
Said it was a shame.
They whipped and they stripped
And they hung me on high,
And they left me there
On a Cross to die.

Chorus

I danced on a Friday
When the sky turned black—
It's hard to dance
With the devil on your back.
They buried my body
And they thought I'd gone,
But I am the Dance,
And I still go on.

Chorus

They cut me down
And I leapt up high;
I am the life
That'll never, never die;
I'll live in you
If you'll live in me—
I am the Lord
Of the Dance, said he.

Chorus[2]

The Dance of God

If Jesus is a dancer, God the Father also is a dancer. The Spirit dances too. The dance of Jesus is a dimension of the dance of God. If we are imaginative enough, we may see the loving and creative interaction among the three Persons of the Trinity as a never-ending dance. But with regard to us, the dance of God starts with creation. It is a free, gratuitous act. God is giving Godself. The visible—sensible, that is related to the senses—cosmos is the expression, the manifestation of God's gift of love. The universe is dynamic. If each molecule is a never-ending dance of atoms, the whole cosmos is an ever-expanding dance of the planets and the stars. Their dance is creative, giving rise to the process of evolution, as beings become more and more complex. Evolution itself would not be possible if the various elements were not in perfect balance to allow such a creative process. And all through the process of creation God plays. A look at Job 38—41 gives us an inkling of God's play. It is too long to quote here, but a few verses indicate the spirit. Job has lost all his family and property and is himself afflicted with leprosy. Interpreting suffering as punishment, Job challenges God, saying that he has been just and that his suffering is unmerited. But God asserts God's freedom as creator. Even the suffering of Job then becomes the play of God beyond the causal explanations offered by Job and his friends.

> Have you commanded the morning since your days
> began,
> and caused the dawn to know its place,
> so that it might take hold of the skirts of the earth,
> and the wicked be shaken out of it?
> (Jb 38:12–13)

> Where is the way to the dwelling of the light,
> and where is the place of darkness,
> that you may take it to its territory
> and that you may discern the paths to its home?
> (Jb 38:19–20)

> Who has cut a channel for the torrents of rain,
> and a way for the thunderbolt,
> to bring rain on a land where no one lives,
> on the desert, which is empty of human life,
> to satisfy the waste and desolate land,
> and to make the ground put forth grass?
> (Jb 38:25–27)

> Do you give the horse its might?
> Do you cloth its neck with mane?
> Do you make it leap like the locust?
> Its majestic snorting is terrible.

> It paws violently, exults mightily;
>   it goes out to meet the weapons.
> It laughs at fear, and is not dismayed;
>   it does not turn back from the sword. (Jb 39:19–22)

> Is it by your wisdom that the hawk soars,
>   and spreads its wings toward the south?
> Is it at your command that the eagle mounts up
>   and makes its nest on high? (Jb 39:26–27)

We can see God enjoying the turning out of the cosmos, of the birds, and of the animals. It is a pity that God does not go on to describe humans—perhaps, because history is also their play. History becomes a duet between the free action of God and the free response of humans.

God does not need the creation. God creates out of love with a desire to give and to share God's own life. That is why God creates free humans who can respond in love. God watches creation unfolding and the free interaction of humans. Freedom means the possibility of refusal. God does not force God's love and life on anyone. God, however, enables humans to respond creatively. God becomes human in Jesus to further empower them with personal and social support. In ways unknown to us God is gathering all things into a unity (Eph 1:3–10). Christ, of course, has a central place and role in the process. That is why he is part of the dance. "For in him all the fullness of God was pleased to dwell, and through him God was pleased to reconcile to himself all things, whether on earth or in heaven, by making peace through the blood of his cross" (Col 1:19–20). The book of Revelation offers us the final vision:

> Then I saw a new heaven and a new earth . . . And I heard a loud voice from the throne saying, "See, the home of God is among the mortals. He will dwell with them as their God; they will be his peoples, and God himself will be with them; he will wipe every tear from their eyes. Death will be no more; mourning and crying and pain will be no more, for the first things have passed away." And the one who was seated on the throne said, "See, I am making all things new." (Rv 21:1, 3–5)

In another situation or culture the author would have added: "And they were all dancing for joy and fulfillment." Paul affirms that the whole of creation is participating in this process:

> For the creation waits with eager longing for the revealing of the children of God; for the creation was subjected to futility, not of its own

will but by the will of the one who subjected it, in hope that the creation itself will be set free from its bondage to decay and will obtain the freedom of the glory of the children of God. We know that the whole creation has been groaning in labor pains until now; and not only the creation, but we ourselves, who have the firstfruits of the Spirit, groan inwardly while we wait for adoption, the redemption of our bodies. (Rom 8:19–23)

The Spirit Is Dancing

This brings us to the role of the Spirit in the cosmic dance. The Spirit is there at the beginning when creation starts its dance. The book of Genesis says: "In the beginning when God created the heavens and the earth, the earth was a formless void and darkness covered the face of the deep, while the spirit of God swept over the face of the waters" (Gn 1:1–2). So the Spirit inaugurates the dancing movement of the cosmos. The people's sins and selfishness make it a dance of death. So God promises them the spirit of new life: "A new heart I will give you, and a new spirit I will put within you; and I will remove from your body the heart of stone and give you a heart of flesh" (Ez 36:26). This spirit will transform a valley of dry bones into a living community (Ez 37:1–14). The Spirit hovers over Jesus and makes his ministry effective (Lk 1:35; 3:22; 4:18). Jesus breathes on the apostles after his resurrection and gives them the spirit of reconciliation and freedom (Jn 20:22–23). The Spirit dances as tongues of fire on the apostles on the day of Pentecost, and they break out into different languages (Acts 1:3–4). The Spirit is the source of freedom and creativity in the community and in the cosmos (Rom 8), and this is a source of harmony, since "all things work together for good for those who love God" (Rom 8:28). The Spirit gives various charisms to the community, so that it can be built up as a community of love and harmony (1 Cor 12—13).

Dance and Suffering

Imagining the whole of creation dancing, we cannot ignore the elements of decay, pain, and suffering in the world. Looked at in themselves they can seem negative. But in the overall cosmic process they are moments of transformation in a necessary evolution. This is true also of suffering caused by humans. We can protect ourselves from suffering as far as possible. But when suffering seems inevitable, we have to respond to it in a human and positive way with creative, nonviolent love. God gives us an example of it. So does Jesus. Let us take a look at the example of Jesus, briefly, since we have spoken about this elaborately in an earlier chapter.

Jesus certainly does not go after suffering as a value in itself. He stands for values like freedom, love, and justice. He sides with the poor and the oppressed in the world—the people who are at the receiving end of a dominant relationship. He foresees that this will lead him to an encounter with the powers that be and that he will have to suffer, even die. He not only stands firm on his values but launches a people's movement to promote them in the world. So he faces his suffering and death with courage and love. His suffering will challenge even his oppressors to conversion. His suffering is redemptive, because it enables love, which expresses itself as humble service and self-gift. Loving unto death is a radical gesture that provokes a radical response both from his followers and his enemies. By facing suffering and death Jesus also shows that they are not the end of life. Jesus rises again. Life continues. Suffering becomes part of a creative process in a world where liberties confront each other. Just as players in a game make strenuous efforts to play and to win, pain and suffering become part of the effort to live and to build community.

God could have created a different human world. But having created humans free, suffering imposed by some on others becomes inevitable. I wonder whether a world of human robots instead of free humans would have been better. It is said that an Indian king went to watch a football match. He saw twenty-two players running after a single ball. So he ordered his minister to give each player a ball. But with each player running after his own ball, there is no game. Once we have a world of free humans thrown onto a single field to interact, the challenge is how to play the game, how to meet suffering in a creative way, and how to build community.

The dance of humanity and creation continues also through pain and suffering. It is the dance of life. That is why Jesus dances, not only at his resurrection, but also on the cross. It is true that Jesus prayed, "Abba, Father, remove this cup from me" (Mk 14:36). It is true that he cried, "My God, my God why have you forsaken me" (Mk 15:34). But he also says, "Father, forgive them; for they do not know what they are doing" (Lk 23:24). Then he offers himself, "Father, into your hands I commend my spirit." But this offering is preceded by as sense of accomplishment—"It is finished" (Jn 19:30).

What we see in the passion of Jesus is that, in spite of all the suffering, Jesus is calm and a master of himself. He must have enjoyed an inner peace and the satisfaction of doing the will of the Father and of accomplishing the task that the Father had given him. He also hopes that God will vindicate him. This must have been a source of deep joy even as he was hanging on the cross. Jesus on the cross is not the victim but the hero. He does not deserve our commiseration and pity but our congratulations and admiration. We should not cry for him but dance with him. Suffering too becomes an element in the cosmic dance.

In the Hindu tradition the favorite places where the Nataraja dances are the burial ground and the hearts of his devotees. The burial ground, of course, is linked to death. But his devotees argue that only a person who can create can destroy. Destruction in the hands of a creator can never be ultimate; it is only a passage, a transformation, a moment of creation. The hearts in which the Nataraja dances live through every transformation, while the dance continues. Death, life, and love are closely linked.

Dance and Freedom

If Jesus danced at death it was because he was dancing through life. He lived as a free being, unencumbered by the legal prescriptions followed by the Pharisees. He questioned their rules about pure and impure foods, and pure and impure persons to relate to. He challenged their interpretation of the sabbath observance. He freely wandered around the lake front and the countryside. He saw the trees grow and the flowers bloom. He watched the birds fly around in the air and the fish moving around the sea. He observed the billowing waves of the sea and the boats of the fishermen dancing on their crests. He felt the cool breeze in the quiet emptiness of the night in desert places and on mountaintops. He felt free to associate with tax collectors and sinners. He felt at liberty to reinterpret authoritatively the tradition of the ancients. He freed the Temple courts from buyers and sellers. He walked on the water. He raised the dead to life. He forgave sins and freed people from guilt. He liberated people from illness and oppression. In short, Jesus lived as a free person, free to relate to nature, free to relate to God without the mediation of ritual structures, and free to relate to others without being hindered by social taboos.

But what is really important is that he freed the people who came to him. He showed by his miracles that bodily illness and even phenomena like possession are really the consequence of sin and guilt, not as their punishment, but as their physical and/or psychological manifestion. So he not only healed them physically, but at the same time he freed them spiritually by releasing them from sin and guilt. There are many symbolic events in his life. While he is talking to a crowd in a house they bring him a paralytic and lower him, still on his bed, through the roof. The first words Jesus speaks to him are these: "Take heart, son; your sins are forgiven." The scribes present accuse him of blasphemy, because God alone can forgive sins. Then Jesus goes on to say: "Stand up, take your bed and go to your home" (Mt 9:2–8). The physical healing simply makes visible the spiritual healing through forgiveness of sins. The sick person must have jumped up and danced for joy.

Another event concerns a sinful woman. Jesus is in the house of a Pharisee who is playing host. A sinful woman comes, washes his feet with her tears, and wipes them with her hair. Jesus explains to the Pharisee, "Her sins, which were many, have been forgiven; hence she has shown great love" (Lk 7:47). It is worth noting that forgiveness precedes love. This is an example of what is called the prevenient love of God: that is, God loves us first before we respond to God in love.

The parable of the Good Shepherd and the parable of the Prodigal Father (Lk 15) show God as loving and forgiving. The same theme is evoked when Jesus sits at table with tax collectors and sinners and responds to the protesting Pharisees by quoting scripture: "I desire mercy, not sacrifice" (Mt 9:10–13).

Many of the cases of possession may really indicate social oppression of various kinds (Mt 8:28–34). Jesus also demands faith both from those who wish to be healed (Mt 8:10; 9:22, 28; 15:28) and from those who wish to heal (Mt 17:14–21). This suggests that the root of sickness and possession is lack of faith or a right relationship with God. Once this relationship is restored, healing follows.

Jesus frees people by reinterpreting the law and insisting on right attitudes. He demands interior commitment rather than external behavior alone (Mt 5—6). A particular instance of this is the healing of the sick on the sabbath, when Jesus stresses that "the sabbath was made for humankind, and not humankind for the sabbath" (Mk 2:27).

By calming the storm Jesus may also have calmed the fear of the disciples as they are taken up by the activism of Jesus (Mk 4:35–41). By reaching out to the Samaritans through one of their women (Jn 4:1–42), to tax collectors like Matthew, whom he calls to become his disciple (Mt 9:9), and to Zacchaeus, who commits himself to justice (Lk 19:1–10), Jesus is empowering the socially marginalized, freeing them at the same time from rigid ritual institutions. He tells the Samaritan woman, "The hour is coming and is now here, when the true worshipers will worship the Father in spirit and truth" (Jn 4:23). I can imagine that the Samaritan woman in her village, Matthew in his house, and Zacchaeus in his community organized celebrations with singing and dancing.

Jesus is dancing through life, leading the people in dance and healing them and making them whole, freeing them from social and religious institutions that oppress. Many of the people who were healed must have danced for joy. This joy reaches its climax when the crowd leads him into Jerusalem, with branches in their hands, shouting: "Hosanna to the Son of David! Blessed is the one who comes in the name of the Lord! Hosanna in the highest heaven!" (Mt 21:9). It is difficult to imagine the people marching in an orderly procession. They surely must have been singing and dancing. The only people who could not dance were the high priests and the Pharisees, who were weighed down with their own self-importance, self-centeredness, and lust for power.

Dancing and Harmony

Just as dancing promotes and achieves self-integration, Jesus encourages personal harmony. In his Sermon on the Mount he suggests not only that inner intentions are more important than external behavior, but that action must correspond to intention (Mt 5:21—6:24). It is not enough to refrain from murder and adultery. We must avoid the desires and tendencies to such actions. Almsgiving, prayer, and fasting must express inner attitudes and not be mere external show. Jesus suggests a harmony between interiority and action.

Fragmentation in the community and oppression are the results of self-ishness and hatred. Where love replaces hatred and self-giving displaces egotism, there is harmony and peace. Jesus lives and promotes harmony at various levels. Jesus announces forgiving and serving love of others as his new commandment and thereby promotes community and social harmony. He radicalizes this demand by asking his disciples to love their enemies and by proposing his Father as a model (Mt 5:48).

A similar harmony must also exist between us and God. When someone told him, "Look, your mother and your brothers are standing outside, want-ing to speak to you," Jesus replied, pointing to the disciples, "Here are my mother and my brothers! For whoever does the will of my Father in heaven is my brother and sister and mother" (Mt 12:47–50). This union with God (and with himself) is expressed in terms of total self-gift. Jesus gives paradoxi-cal expression to it. He says: "Whoever loves father or mother more than me is not worthy of me; and whoever loves son or daughter more than me is not worthy of me; and whoever does not take up the cross and follow me is not worthy of me. Those who find their life will lose it, and those who lose their life for my sake will find it" (Mt 10:37–39). It is this same attitude of total self-gift to God and total dependence on God that finds expression in the Beatitudes:

> "Blessed are you who are poor,
>   for yours is the kingdom of God.
> Blessed are you who are hungry now,
>   for you will be filled.
> Blessed are you who weep now,
>   for you will laugh." (Lk 6:20–21)

In his own life Jesus experiences this oneness with the Father. He tells the disciples, "No one knows the Son except the Father; and no one knows the

Father except the Son and anyone to whom the Son chooses to reveal him" (Mt 11:27). He says further, "Whoever has seen me has seen the Father" (Jn 14:9). Or again, "The Father and I are one" (Jn 10:30). This union is manifested in the fact that Jesus does the will of his Father (Jn 10:37–38). Doing the will of the Father leads Jesus to a total emptying of himself (Phil 2:7–8). He prays in the garden, "Not my will but yours be done" (Lk 22:42).

Jesus extends this fellowship with God also to the disciples: "Those who love me will keep my word, and my Father will love them, and we will come to them and make our home with them" (Jn 14:23). This makes a mutual indwelling and harmony possible between us and God: "That they may all be one. As you, Father, are in me and I am in you, may they also be in us" (Jn 17:21). The Spirit of God is also included in this communion: "If you love me, you will keep my commandments. And I will ask my Father, and he will give you another Advocate, to be with you for ever. This is the Spirit of truth" (Jn 14:15–17).

Such a harmony within oneself, with others, with Jesus, with the Spirit, and with the Father is the source of peace (Jn 16:33) and joy (Jn 16:24) and creativity (Jn 14:12). Jesus promises that "those who abide in me and I in them bear much fruit" (Jn 15:5). This harmony, therefore, is not static, focused on being, but dynamic, shown in doing. It can be seen as a creative harmony in movement or dance. Jesus is not only the dancer, but he makes the whole world dance.

11

Jesus,
the Pilgrim

In India there is a tradition of praising God with 1,001 names. Christians have compiled litanies of 1,001 names for Jesus too. These names normally consist either of an indication of his personal qualities or of a reference to his life and actions. I am not going to evoke these 1,001 names. I have explored seven images in the foregoing pages. I think that they are representative. They can evoke devotion and discipleship. I would like to conclude this contemplation of Asian images of Jesus with a final one on Jesus as a pilgrim.

Pilgrimage is a popular *sadhana* or religious practice even today. People who would not normally go regularly to a church or a temple may go on a pilgrimage. The goal of a pilgrimage is to visit a place where God has chosen to self-manifest in power, revealing, healing, or granting favors. People hope to encounter God, experience God's presence. They prepare themselves by doing penance, making themselves worthy of receiving divine self-manifestation. Part of this penance is to walk to the sacred place, fasting and praying. Pilgrims normally go as a group, inspiring and encouraging one another. Common devotion to God ties them together into a community that crosses the boundaries of social divisions. The place of pilgrimage is a goal but not an end. Having encountered the Divine, people come back to life with a new purpose and a new vigor to live their experience in the world. Further, people tend to repeat pilgrimages. And pilgrimage is found in all religions. One of the five pillars of Islam is a pilgrimage to Mecca at least once in a person's lifetime, if possible. Pilgrimages to the Holy Land or to other sacred spots like Lourdes are common in Christianity. Pilgrimages to sacred mountains, rivers, and images are frequent in Hinduism. Buddhists come to Bodhgaya, the place of Buddha's enlightenment.

Some stories in the Bible can be seen as pilgrimages. Abraham leaves his native place and goes in search of the land that God promises him. The Israelites leave Egypt and spend forty years walking toward the promised land.

In the promised land Jerusalem becomes the holy place where they go on pilgrimage periodically, every year if possible. When they are driven into exile, one of their regrets is their inability to go to Jerusalem.

In the gospels Luke presents Jesus and his followers as pilgrims. The public life of Jesus is presented as the journey of Jesus toward Jerusalem. This journey ends in death. His resurrection shows that death is not the final event but only a passage. After his death and resurrection Jesus sends his disciples to the ends of the earth. The story of the journey of two disciples to Emmaus, in which Jesus joins them as a fellow pilgrim who enlightens and leads them to a vision of his presence in the breaking of the bread illustrates what this new stage of pilgrimage involves. The disciples had been waiting for the reestablishment of the kingdom of Israel. That hope had been dashed with the death of Jesus. But now Jesus reveals the true goal of their pilgrimage: human community in the world. Pictures of Jesus at Emmaus show him alone with the two disciples. It is quite possible that in an inn there were many others sharing the table at the end of various journeys. The breaking of bread may have been during a shared meal with many people. By manifesting himself in that context Jesus indicates the new goal of pilgrimage—human community. It is in the community that God's presence is manifested. Jesus himself becomes bodily present in the shared meal according to the faith of the Christian community. The goal of the pilgrimage is God. But God is not found in heaven but in the world, in a community of people who love and serve one another, sharing all that they have. The early church realized this. Its members sold everything that they had, shared the proceeds with the community, and celebrated the new fellowship in a shared meal (Acts 2:43–47).

During his lifetime, when Jesus calls people to become his disciples, the request is always to "follow him." When he sends his disciples to proclaim the good news of the kingdom of God, the instructions he gives are suitable to pilgrims (Mt 10): do not carry too much luggage, depend on the hospitality of the people, move on from place to place, keep moving till you find peace, but then carry it on to others.

The Jews were searching and waiting for a messiah who would lead them to the promised kingdom. Jesus comes as the messiah. He does not bring their pilgrimage to an end. On the contrary, he sends them on a new pilgrimage toward the kingdom that will come. That kingdom, however, is being realized in communities of people. Almost as a symbol of this change the temple in Jerusalem will be destroyed a few decades after his own death, forcing the people to look outward.

Paul too is seen as a pilgrim. He comes to Jerusalem from Tarsus. From Jerusalem he goes to Damascus, looking for Christians to capture. His intention is to give glory to God by punishing people who are seen as be-trayers of God's revelation and trust. But enlightened by the Lord in the course of his journey, he changes both his goal and his route. He travels the then-known world, establishing new communities of believers in Jesus. His pilgrimage continues even in prison and ends only with his death.

In such a context the image of Jesus walking with his disciples toward Emmaus becomes the symbol of the pilgrimage that all of us have to under-take. Our lives become a pilgrimage going toward an encounter with God. The disciples going to Emmaus are actually seeking to escape from Jerusa-lem, where unexpected, unpleasant things have happened. But Jesus comes to walk along with them. He dispels their misunderstanding by explaining the scriptures, inspires them so that their hearts are burning, and leads them to an encounter where they recognize the presence of the Lord. Jesus mani-fests his presence, not in thunder, smoke, and lightning, but in the breaking of bread, that is, in a sign of sharing and self-gift.

Our life too is a pilgrimage. We have to walk our way toward divine en-counter. But we do not walk alone. First of all, Jesus walks with us, enlight-ening and empowering us. He leads us to encounter God, not in a sacred place made special by miraculous phenomena, but in the common experi-ence of a shared meal. God is encountered in the world. That is why Jesus sends the disciples not to a new Jerusalem but to the world. The secular becomes the sacred.

Second, as we walk along, we discover that everybody is on a pilgrimage searching for God, while the Spirit of God is empowering them in ways un-known to us. We become co-pilgrims with humanity. We can then share with others the way of Jesus. Jesus is the way. We have seen above what this means. Others, too, will share with us what they have discovered about the way. And all of us are walking together to discover God in the world, in oth-ers. Addressing the leaders of other religions in Chennai in 1986, John Paul II said:

> By dialogue we let God be present in our midst; for as we open our-selves in dialogue with one another, we also open ourselves to God . . . As followers of different religions we should join together in promot-ing and defending common ideals in the spheres of religious liberty, human brotherhood, education, culture, social welfare and civic order.

While preparing for the special Synod of Bishops for Asia, the bishops of the Philippines insisted:

> In the social context of the great majority of Asian peoples, even more use should be made of the model of the Church as servant, a co-pilgrim

in the journey to the Kingdom of God where fullness of life is given as a gift.[1]

And the bishops of Malaysia, Singapore, and Brunei asked: "What can the Church learn from her dialogue with other religions?" and answered:

> From the Muslims, the Church can learn about prayer, fasting and almsgiving.
> From Hindus, the Church can learn about meditation and contemplation.
> From Buddhists, the Church can learn about detachment from material goods and respect for life.
> From Confucianism, the Church can learn about filial piety and respect for elders.
> From Taoism, the Church can learn about simplicity and humility.
> From Animists, the Church can learn about the reverence and respect for nature and gratitude for harvests.
> The Church can learn from their rich symbolism and rites existing in their diversity of worship.
> The Church can, like the Asian religions, learn to be more open, receptive, sensitive, tolerant, and forgiving in the midst of plurality of religions.[2]

Dialogue then becomes an essential ingredient of pilgrimage.

History can be seen as a pilgrimage. The humans and the whole cosmos are on pilgrimage. The goal is the kingdom of God. The kingdom of God is a community, not only of all humans, but also of the cosmos in which God will be "all in all" (1 Cor 15:28). This community is being built up in the course of the pilgrimage. Christ comes into history to become the leader of the pilgrimage. Paul seems particularly aware of this process. He speaks of history as the "gathering of all things" (Eph 1:10) and the "reconciliation of all things" (Col 1:20). He gives Christ a special role in the process as the "firstfruits" (1 Cor 15:23). He sees the Spirit as the inner agent of the process that involves the whole cosmos (Rom 8:9–23). Both Christ and the Spirit are walking along with us in this pilgrimage: Christ as the firstfruits and the leader, and the Spirit as the inner animator. Other images, like Jesus as the light, can be contemplated in this context: "I am the light of the world. Whoever follows me will never walk in darkness but will have the light of life" (Jn 8:12).

Conclusion

If Jesus were to ask us today "Who do you say that I am?" we would probably repeat a dogmatic formula that we were taught in catechism class about his being one of the three Persons in the Trinity, having two natures. Yet, Jesus would not be impressed by our answer, with its presumption to know exactly what he is. The dogmatic formula has its relevance in situations similar to the one in which it was evolved. But the interest Jesus has in asking us the question would be much more like: What do I mean to you? How do I affect the way you live? Is your life better because of your knowledge of me? In the same way, when we ask how Jesus Christ is our savior, the answer we need is not a metaphysical explanation of the process of salvation, though that may be relevant in some circumstances, but how his saving grace is able to transform our lives and enable us to meet its challenges. The saving grace of Jesus does not free us from following Jesus in our lives. Jesus does not save us in some magical way. He enables us to live and love in a new way. He does not take us away from the world. He wants us to get involved in it. He calls us to walk in his way. But he will walk with us, encouraging us. And he will walk before us, leading us.

The images that I have evoked here and others that we find in the gospels and in Christian tradition will inspire us and energize us. It will be helpful, therefore, to contemplate these images. We should not rationalize them. But we should let them act on our imagination and provoke our commitment and conviction to walk with Jesus, to live like him. We should not compare images. Each one has its special appeal in particular situations to particular people at particular times. So we ourselves may move from one to the other in the varying circumstances of our lives.

I do hope that these images will help us to discover the Asian Jesus, to follow him in an Asian way, and to witness to him before other Asians in a meaningful manner. May the Asian Jesus lead all of us to the fullness of God.

Notes

Introduction

1. Of course the terms *West* and *East* are used in relation to Palestine, in which Jesus was born and lived.

2. *East* and *West* here are obviously used to distinguish two regions within the empire.

3. Quoted from *Proposition 6* of the bishops at the Asian Synod by John Paul II in *The Church in Asia,* 20.

4. M. Thomas Thangaraj, *The Crucified Guru: An Experiment in Cross-Cultural Christology* (Nashville, TN: Abingdon Press, 1994).

1 Images of Jesus in Christian History

1. Quoted in Robin Boyd, *An Introduction to Indian Christian Theology* (Delhi: ISPCK, 2000), 77–78.

2 Images of Jesus among Other Asian Believers

1. Quoted in M. M.Thomas, *The Acknowledged Christ of the Indian Renaissance* (Madras: Christian Literature Society, 1970), 9.

2. Sophia Dobson Collet, *The Life and Letters of Raja Ram Mohan Roy* (London, 1900), 42, quoted in ibid.

3. Swami Gambirananda, *The History of the Ramakrishna Math and Mission* (Calcutta, 1957), 16.

4. See S. J. Samartha, *The Hindu Response to the Unbound Christ* (Madras: Christian Literature Society, 1974), 45–46.

5. *The Complete Works of Swami Vivekananda* (Almora, 1931), 7:20, 27.

6. Ibid., 1:22.

7. Ibid., 7:1.

8. Ibid., 4:141ff.

9. M. K. Gandhi, *Harijan*, February 16, 1934, quoted in Samartha, *The Hindu Response to the Unbound Christ,* 80.

10. M. K.Gandhi, *The Message of Jesus Christ* (Bombay, 1940), cover page.

11. Ibid., Preface.

12. Ibid., 79.

13. Ibid., 35.

14. Ibid., 21, 36.

15. *Young India,* December 31, 1931, quoted in Samartha, *The Hindu Response to the Unbound Christ,* 93.

16. Gandhi., *The Message of Jesus Christ,* 6, 140.

17. *The Modern Review,* October 1941, quoted in Samartha, *The Hindu Response to the Unbound Christ,* 94.

18. See Paul Arthur Schilpp, ed., *The Philosophy of Sarvepalli Radhakrishnan* (New York, 1952), 807.

19. Ibid., 79.

20. S. Radhakrishnan, *The Heart of Hinduism* (Madras, 1932), 100.

21. Richard W. Taylor, *Jesus in Indian Painting* (Madras: Christian Literature Society, 1975),

22. K.C.S. Panikkar, quoted in ibid., 72.

23. Nikhil Biswas, quoted in ibid., 79.

24. Arup Das, quoted in ibid., 83.

25. P. Lal, in ibid., 57.

26. See also Buddhadasa, *Un Bouddhiste dit le Christiniasme aux Bouddhistes* (Paris: Desclée, 1987); idem, *Le Dalaï-Lama parle de Jésus* (Paris: Brepols, 1996).

27. Thich Nhat Hanh, *Living Buddha, Living Christ* (London: Rider, 1995), 37–38, 44, 56.

4 Jesus, the Way

1. George Soares-Prabhu, "The Kingdom of God: Jesus' Vision of a New Society," in *Theology of Liberation: An Indian Biblical Perspective,* ed. Francis D'Sa and Scaria Kuthirakkattel (Pune: JDV, 2001), 238–39.

2. Ibid., 244.

7 Jesus, the Avatar

1. Thomas Aquinas, *Summa Theologiae* 3,3,7.

2. See Francis X. Clooney, *Hindu God, Christian God: How Reason Helps Break Down the Boundaries between Religions* (New York: Oxford Univ. Press, 2001), 94–128.

3. Robin Boyd, *An Introduction to Indian Christian Theology* (Delhi: ISPCK, 2000), 115.

4. Ibid., 116.

5. Ibid., 116–17.

10 Jesus, the Dancer

1. Sara Grant, *The Lord of the Dance* (Bangalore: Asian Trading Corporation, 1987), 195.

2. "Lord of the Dance," lyrics by Sydney Carter; melody adapted from a 19th century Shaker tune (London: Stainer & Bell; Carol Stream, Illinois: Hope Publishing Company, 1963).

11 Jesus, the Pilgrim

1. Peter C. Phan, ed., *The Asian Synod: Text and Commentaries* (Maryknoll, NY: Orbis Books, 2002), 39.

2. Ibid., 36.

Select Bibliography

Ainger, Geoffrey. *Jesus Our Contemporary.* New York: Seabury Press, 1967.

Alangaram, A. *Christ of the Asian Peoples.* Bangalore: Asian Trading Corporation, 2001.

Amaladoss, Michael. "The Image of Jesus in *The Church in Asia.*" *Jeevadhara* 30 (2000), 281-90; *East Asian Pastoral Review* 37 (2000), 233-41.

———. "Images of Christ and Orientations in Mission: A Historical Overview." *Vidyajyoti Journal of Theological Reflection* 61 (1997), 732-41.

———. "Images of Jesus in India." In *De ene Jezus en de vele culturen: Christologie en contentualiteit,* ed. Nico Schreurs and Huub van de Sandt, 23-36. Tilburg: Univ. Press, 1992; *East Asian Pastoral Review* 31 (1994), 6-20.

———. "Jésus-Christ en Asie: Exploration Préliminaire." *Mission de l'Église,* Supplément du N° 124 (1999), 4-16.

———. "La Réponse indienne à Jésus." *Jésus sans Frontières.* Hors Series 4. Paris: L'Actualité Religeiuse dans le Monde, Dossiers Chauds (1994), 5–7.

Andrews, C. F. "The Hindu View of Christ." *International Review for Mission* 28 (1939).

Arockiasamy, Soosai. *Dharma, Hindu and Christian, according to Robert de Nobili.* Documenta Missionalia Series 19. Rome: Editrice Pontificia Universita Gregoriana, 1986.

Badrinath, Chaturvedi. *Finding Jesus in Dharma: Christianity in India.* Delhi: ISPCK, 2000.

Bonino, José Mígues, ed. *Faces of Jesus: Latin American Christologies.* Maryknoll, NY: Orbis Books, 1984.

Borg, Marcus J. *Jesus, a New Vision: Spirit, Culture, and the Life of Discipleship.* San Francisco: Harper, 1987.

———, ed. *Jesus at 2000.* Boulder, CO: Westview Press, 1998.

Boyd, Robin. *An Introduction to Indian Christian Theology.* Delhi: ISPCK, 2000.

Brown, Raymond E. *An Introduction to New Testament Christology.* London: Geoffrey Chapman, 1994.

Chenchiah, P. "The Vedanta Philosophy and the Message of Christ." *Indian Journal of Theology* 4, no. 2 (1955).

Clooney, Francis X. *Hindu God, Christian God: How Reason Helps Break Down the Boundaries between Religions.* New York: Oxford Univ. Press, 2001.

Cullmann, Oscar. *The Christology of the New Testament.* Philadelphia: Westminster Press, 1963.

Dalai-Lama. *Le Dalaï-Lama parle de Jésus.* Paris: Brepols, 1996.

Damascene, Hieromonk. *Christ the Eternal Tao.* Platina: Valaam Books, 2002.

De Andia, Ysabel, and Peter Leander Hofrichter, eds. *Christus be den Vätern.* Innsbruck: Tirolia, 2004.

Devdas, Nalini. "The Christ of the Ramakrishna Movement." *Religion and Society* 11, no. 3 (September 1964).

D'Lima, Errol, and Max Gonsalves, eds. *What Does Jesus Christ Mean? The Meaning of Jesus Christ and Religious Pluralism in India.* Bangalore: Indian Theological Association, 1999.

Douglas, Kelly Brown. *The Black Christ.* Maryknoll, NY: Orbis Books, 2001.

Edwards, Denis. *Jesus and the Wisdom of God.* Maryknoll, NY: Orbis Books, 1995.

Ehrman Bart D. *Jesus: Apocalyptic Prophet of the New Millennium.* New York: Oxford Univ. Press, 1999.

Endo, Shusaku. *A Life of Jesus.* Mahwah, NJ: Paulist Press, 1973.

Falvey, Lindsay. *The Buddha's Gospel: A Buddhist Interpretation of Jesus' Words.* Adelaide: Institute for International Development, 2002.

Fédou, Michel. *Regards asiatiques sur le Christ.* Paris: Desclée, 1998.

———, ed. *Le Fils unique et ses frères: Unicité du Christ et pluralisme religieux.* Paris: Editions faculté jésuites, 2002.

Fiorenza, Elisabeth Schüssler. *Jesus: Miriam's Child, Sophia's Prophet.* New York: Continuum, 1995.

———. *Jesus and the Politics of Interpretation.* New York: Continuum, 2001.

In God's Image 22, no. 4 (December 2003). The theme for this issue is "Christ for Asian Women."

Grün, Anselm. *Images of Jesus.* Mumbai: St. Paul's, 2002..

Harrington, Wilfred. *The Jesus Story.* Collegeville, MN: Liturgical Press, 1991.

Hoffmann, R. Joseph. *Jesus outside the Gospels.* Buffalo, NY: Prometheus Books, 1984.

Hospital, Clifford G. "The Contribution of Keshub Chunder Sen toward a Global and Inductive Christology." *Journal of Ecumenical Studies* 19, no. 1 (Winter 1982).

Jeyaraj D. "The Contribution of the Catholic Church in Tamilnadu in the 17th-19th Centuries to an Understanding of Christ." *Indian Journal of Theology* 23 (1974).

Keenan, John P. *The Meaning of Christ: A Mahayana Theology.* Maryknoll, NY: Orbis Books, 1989.

Küster, Volker. *The Many Faces of Jesus Christ.* Maryknoll, NY: Orbis Books, 2001.

La Due, William J. *Jesus among the Theologians: Contemporary Interpretations of Christ.* Harrisburg, PA: Trinity Press International, 2001.

Lee, Bernard J. *Jesus and the Metaphors of God: The Christs of the New Testament.* New York: Paulist Press, 1993.

Malek, Roman, ed. *The Chinese Face of Jesus Christ.* 2 vols. Sankt Augustin: Institut Monumenta Serica and China-Zentrum, 2002, 2003.

Mattam, Joseph. "Modern Catholic Attempts at Presenting Christ to India." *Indian Journal of Theology* 23 (1974).

Meyendorf, John. *Christ in Eastern Christian Thought.* Washington: Corpus Books, 1969.

Miles, Jack. *Christ: A Crisis in the Life of God.* New York: Vintage Books, 2001.

Nhat Hanh, Thich. *Living Buddha, Living Christ.* London: Rider, 1995

O'Grady, John F. *Models of Jesus Revisited.* New York: Paulist Press, 1994.

O'Grady, Ron, ed. *Christ for All People: Celebrating a World of Christian Art.* Maryknoll, NY: Orbis Books, 2001.

Palmer, Martin. *The Jesus Sutras: Rediscovering the Lost Religion of Taoist Christianity.* London: Piatkus, 2001.

Panikkar, Raimon. *Christophany: The Fullness of Man.* Maryknoll, NY: Orbis Books, 2004.

Paradkar, Balwant A. M. "Hindu Interpretation of Christ from Vivekananda to Radhakrishnan." *Indian Journal of Theology* 18 (1969).

Parapally, Jacob. *Emerging Trends in Indian Christology.* Bangalore: IIS Publications, 1995.

Pelikan, Jaroslav. *Jesus through the Centuries: His Place in the History of Culture.* New York: Harper and Row, 1987.

Pieris, Aloysius. "The Christhood of Jesus." *Logos* 39, no. 3 (2000): 1-70.

Porter, Stanley E., Michael A. Hayes, and David Tombs, eds. *Images of Christ Ancient and Modern.* Sheffield: Sheffield Academic Press, 1997.

Rajan, P. Swarnalata. "Christian Dalit Aspirations as Expressed by Jashuva Kavi in Gabbilam (the Bat)." *Religion and Society* 34, no. 3.

Santram, Philip J. "Christ of the Brahmo Samaj Movement." *Religion and Society* 11, no. 3 (September 1964).

Schillebeeckx, Edward. *Jesus in Our Western Culture: Mysticism, Ethics and Politics.* London: SCM, 1987.

Schreiter, Robert J., ed. *Faces of Jesus in Africa.* Maryknoll, NY: Orbis Books, 1991.

Schwager, Raymund. *Jesus of Nazareth: How He Understood His Life.* New York: Crossroad, 1998.

Senécal, Bernard. *Jésus le Christ à la rencontre de Gautama le Bouddha.* Paris: Cerf, 1998.

Sloyan, Gerard S. *The Jesus Tradition: Images of Jesus in the West.* Mystic, CT: Twenty-third Publications, 1986.

Sugirtharajah, R. S., ed. *Asian Faces of Jesus.* Maryknoll, NY: Orbis Books, 1993.

Thangaraj, M. Thomas. *The Crucified Guru—An Experiment in Cross-Cultural Christology.* Nashville, TN: Abingdon Press, 1994.

Thangasamy, D. A. "Pandipeddi Chenchiah's Understanding of Jesus Christ." *Religion and Society* 11, no. 3 (September 1964).

Thomas, Daniel. "What Jesus Meant to Gandhi." *Religion and Society* 11, no. 3 (September 1964).

Thomas, M. M. *The Acknowledged Christ of Indian Renaissance.* Madras: CLS, 1970.

Vaiharai 7, no. 4 (2002). The theme for this issue is "Indian Faces of Jesus."

Vermander, Benoît. *Le Christ chinois. Héritage et espérance.* Paris: Desclée de Brouwer, 1998.

Witherington, Ben, III. *The Jesus Quest: The Third Search for the Jew of Nazareth.* Downers Grove, IL: InterVarsity Press, 1997.

———. *Jesus the Sage: The Pilgrimage of Wisdom.* Minneapolis: Fortress Press, 2000.

———. *The Many Faces of the Christ: The Christology of the New Testament and Beyond.* New York: Crossroad, 1998.

Scripture Index

Index

Abishiktananda (Swami), 7
advaita, 22, 30, 55–56, 64, 69, 129–30
affirmations, limitations of, 5
ahisma, 24
apostolic social movement, Jesus as guru of, 75–76
Aquinas, Thomas, 107, 121
artha, 31, 56
asanas, 31
asceticism, 66
ashram, 84
avatar: common image of, 105, 116–19, 121; new meaning for, in Christian context, 120–21; specific meaning of, for Jesus, 6–7. *See also* Jesus, as avatar
avatara, 26
avidya, 23

Bhagavad Gita, 49, 56
bhakti, 30, 55
Bharatanatyam, 147, 150
Bharathi, 118
Bible: dancing in, 148; wisdom books in, 31
Biswas, Nikhil, 26
bodhisattva, 75, 135
Bosco, John, 85
brahmacarya, 24
Brahman, 30, 130
Buddha, 27, 85; compassionate nature of, 135; eightfold path of, 56–57
Buddhadasa, Bhikku, 2, 129
Buddhism, recommending detachment, 49

Caitanya, 147
chakras, 30–31
Chenchiah, Pandipeddi, 7
Christ: manifestations of, 107–8; personal experience of, 22; as yogi and *jivanmukta*, 23–24. *See also* Jesus

Christianity: early Eastern presence of, 1; learning from other religions, 164; modern movement into East, response to, 1–2; political structure of, 132–33; western spread of, 1
church, as symbol and servant, 133
communion, 39, 63–65
community building, 58–59, 60, 65, 76–79, 96, 147
comparisons, unnecessary, for studying Jesus, 2–4
compassion, 135–36, 146
Confucians, impressions of Taoists, 54–55
Confucius, 30, 54, 85
Constitution on the Sacred Liturgy (Sacrosanctum Concilium), 107
Coomaraswamy, Ananda, 150
Council of Chalcedon, 5, 16, 115–16
Council of Nicea, 16
cross, as sign of victory, 99–100

Dalai Lama, 2
dance: as collective self-expression, 147–49; freedom and, 157–59; of God, 152–55; harmony and, 159–60; openness to, in liturgy, 148; promoting self-integration, 159; significance of, 149–50; of Spirit, 155; suffering and, 155–57; yin/yang symbolic of, 148
Das, Arup, 26–27
de Nobili, Roberto, 6, 105
dervishes, 147
detachment, 49
dharma, 30, 31, 56
dialogue, 102–3, 164
discernment, Jesus' teachings about, 42–43
disciples, 69–70. *See also* Jesus, disciples of
discipleship, demands of, 79–80

176